Karate Ideals

By
Randall G. Hassell

EMPIRE Books

P.O. Box 491788, Los Angeles, CA 90049

Disclaimer

Please note that the author and publisher of this book are NOT RESPONSIBLE in any manner whatsoever for any injury that may result from practicing the techniques and/or following the instructions given within. Since the physical activities described herein may be too strenuous in nature for some readers to engage in safely, it is essential that a physician be consulted prior to training.

Published in 2006 by Empire Books.

Copyright © 2006 by Randall Hassell

Library of Congress Number: 2006010641
ISBN-10: 1-933901-06-3
ISBN-13: 978-1-933901-06-0

Library of Congress Cataloging-in-Publication Data

Hassell, Randall G.
Karate ideals / by Randall G. Hassell. -- 1st ed. p. cm.
Previously published: St. Louis : Focus Publications, c1995.
Includes index.
ISBN 1-933901-06-3 (pbk. : alk. paper)
1. Karate--Philosophy. 2. Karate--Psychology. I. Title.
GV1114.3.H396 2006
20060106

Empire Books
P.O. Box 491788.
Los Angeles, CA 90049
(818) 767-9000

06 05 04 03 02 01 00 99 98 97 1 3 5 7 9 10 8 6 4 2

Printed in the United States of America

Contents

Acknowledgments

Friends and foes alike help all writers with their work. Friends encourage us directly, and foes unwittingly encourage us to show them that we can. I am grateful to all these people.

In particular, I extend sincere thanks to the late A. R. (Dick) Allen, the Master of Masters, for keeping the faith when I had none left; to Jim Nail for his editorial acumen; and most of all to Marilyn, for making it all seem worthwhile.

About the Author

Martial Arts Illustrated magazine called Randall G. Hassell "Shotokan's Great Communicator" and "The spiritual voice for a generation of karate-do practitioners." *The Fighter International* magazine said Hassell is, "hands down, the world's finest, most authoritative karate-do writer."

Chief Instructor of the American Shotokan Karate Alliance (ASKA), President of the American JKA Karate Association International (AJKA-I), and Senior Editor of Tamashii Press, Randall Hassell is a professional writer and editor who began karate training in 1960. He also is a first generation American to pioneer Shotokan karate, introducing it to the St. Louis, Missouri area in 1961.

While majoring in English Literature at Washington University in St. Louis, he began an intense, formal study of the history and philosophy of the martial arts in general, and karate-do in particular.

To date, this study has led to the publication of more than 100 articles in numerous periodicals around the world, and more than 28 books including:

The Complete Idiot's Guide to Karate; Recognition: A Karate Novel (with Stan Schmidt); *The Karate Experience: A Way of Life; Conversations with the Master: Masatoshi Nakayama; Shotokan Karate: Its History and Evolution; Karate Ideals; The Karate Spirit ; Karate Training Guide Volume 1: Foundations of Training; Karate Training Guide Volume 2: Kata—Heian, Tekki, Bassai Dai; Samurai Journey* (with Osamu Ozawa).

In addition to teaching in his own *dojo* and at various YMCAs and school districts in the St. Louis, Missouri metro area, Mr. Hassell oversees the instruction and administration of thousands of students nationwide in ASKA and AJKA affiliated clubs, and he travels extensively, teaching, lecturing, and officiating.

Foreword

Karate Ideals is a revised collection of numerous articles that have generated a great deal of mail, both pro and con, to the author. Since some of these articles continue to generate interest and debate, I have collected them together, revised them, and added to them to produce *Karate Ideals*.

When I began writing many of the materials in this book in the 1970s, I was a young follower of my Japanese teachers, but in 1984, the world of karate changed drastically around me and around my peers and seniors. After more than 25 years of blind following, we banded together with a single purpose—to promote and support American JKA karate in America. ("JKA" refers to the particular method of the style of Shotokan karate developed by the Japan Karate Association in Japan.)

In October 1984, we formed the American JKA Karate Associations (AJKA) to fulfill our purpose. We were saddened by the fact that a number of our Japanese instructors did not share our view of karate and its future in America, but we were heartened by the fact that some Japanese masters and more than 5,000 American JKA karate-ka did share our view.

Today, while many of us have gone our separate ways and into even more organizations, we still are moving forward in our campaign to strengthen karate in America, and we are very happy that so many people have joined us in our quest.

I wondered if the material in this book, some of which was written while I was a young follower of the Japanese teachers, would have to be changed to reflect the American viewpoint. As I re-read it, however, I was pleased to discover that nothing had to be changed.

The truth of karate-do is still the same, and it transcends all boundaries—ethnic, racial, sexual, organizational, and societal.

Karate is, after all, a Japanese art, and it must be explained in Japanese terms to make sense.

The articles on Masatoshi Nakayama, Hiroshi Shirai, and Takeshi Oishi are as valid now, I believe, as they were when I first wrote them. The lives and thoughts of these extraordinary men challenge the imagination and inspire us to look deeper into our art and ourselves as human beings.

Randall G. Hassell
St. Louis, Missouri

Introduction

The rank examination was over, and we were milling around the *dojo*, waiting for instructions on what to do next. The highest-ranking Japanese masters of JKA Shotokan karate-do in America had been brought to the Midwest for the first large tournament of its kind in Missouri, and we were all in awe of seeing so many of these men gathered in one room. I had recently reached the *shodan* (first degree black belt) level, and I was primarily responsible for the organization and conduct of the coming tournament. It was my job, therefore, to greet these men as they disembarked from their planes, and it was my responsibility to see to it that their needs were met. We had arranged this ranking examination at the *dojo* for the day before the tournament, and more than 30 people had come from around the Midwest to be examined and critiqued by our rare assemblage of masters.

The *dojo* had two *makiwara* (padded punching posts). Each *makiwara* had a base constructed of half-inch steel, two sturdy, welded supports rising 18 inches above a base plate that was 18 inches square.

Quarter-inch holes had been drilled in the base plate, and 12, six-inch steel bolts ran through these holes, through the floor to the basement ceiling, where another 18-inch square plate was matched to the one above. One-inch steel washers and 3/4-inch steel nuts tied the plates together through the floor, making a tight, secure sandwich of steel and oak flooring. The upper part of the *makiwara* consisted of two, one-inch by six-inch maple boards, separated and supported half-way up by a two-by-four. All of us had punched and kicked those *makiwara* hundreds of times every day, and we were convinced they would last forever.

One of the masters, Takayuki Mikami, seventh degree black belt and former All Japan Karate Champion, had pushed on the heavy pad of the *makiwara* before the examination and had pronounced the whole structure "a little stiff."

Now the test was over, and Mikami gave the *makiwara* a double-take as he passed by. I watched as he pushed it, squeezed it, stepped back from it and lowered his hips. He stepped forward quickly and stopped his punch just short of contact with the pad. This he did several times before moving close to the *makiwara*, left leg forward in his long front stance, right fist at the ready on his hip. He punched then, once, twice. Before the third punch, he paused, inhaled deeply, and let out a sharp grunt from the pit of his stomach as his right fist fired forward. The maple board on the front snapped like a toothpick, and the back board split into three pieces with a resounding crack. "Oh-oh," he said apologetically, turning toward me. "Very sorry," he said, handing me the pieces of wood. I assured him it was okay, that the *makiwara* was very old and destined to die soon anyway.

Hidetaka Nishiyama, eighth degree black belt and chief examiner, had not seen any of this, having been busy tallying the scores of the examination. Now, with his clipboard under his left arm, he was walking toward the front of the *dojo*, joking and laughing with another of the masters. As he passed the remaining *makiwara*, he made an odd movement with his hips and smacked the unsuspecting *makiwara* with a thudding back-fist strike, still laughing, and continued without pause toward the front of the *dojo*.

When we examined the remains of his destruction, we found that while the boards on the second *makiwara* had held up admirably, at least three inches of threads on each of the front bolts had been stripped, and three bolts in the rear were bent!

That two men of slight build (Nishiyama was the larger of the two at five feet, seven inches and about 155 pounds) could generate such power under any circumstances would have been sufficient to put us all in a state of shock; that they did it at will, with seeming nonchalance, defied all logic and reason.

How could these men do such things? Would we ever be able to do the same? It must be magic.

The Great Missouri *Makiwara* Massacre occurred in 1968, and in the ensuing years, I have learned that what Masters Nishiyama and Mikami did had nothing at all to do with magic. The only thing mysterious about it was that human beings would devote themselves so completely to their training to attain such high levels. What they displayed was a near-perfect coordination of body and mind—a complete "connection," as Nishiyama called it.

Indeed, it was in that very same week that Nishiyama and Teruyuki Okazaki, another high-ranking master, gave us a series of lectures, the like of which we had not imagined before. Power and strength, they taught us, are not simply the result of extremely strong muscles. Power and strength can be explained scientifically, for the most part, in terms of physics, kinesiology, and mathematics. They taught us that if we were to find true perfection of character and a higher level of existence through karate-do, we first must seek perfection of coordination, raising our bodies and minds to their highest states.

Thus began a long and intense study of body mechanics, conducted by hundreds of students and instructors who sought to find the most efficient methods of body motion in JKA Shotokan karate-do. At the outset, we expected to make great breakthroughs and discover new techniques. What we found, first to our surprise and later to our satisfaction, was that it would take at least 20 or 30 years to merely analyze the techniques as they already existed.

What we have come to today, with the help of karate masters and several scientists and experts in other fields of endeavor, is a rational, scientific view of JKA Shotokan karate-do. It is, we have found, eminently possible and beneficial to draw upon the expertise of others in other fields to supplement our karate training, and from this cooperative effort, to devise modern, scientific training methods that enable karate students to progress faster in the mechanics of their art than their predecessors of even 10 or 15 years ago.

What the karate masters displayed when they broke our *makiwara*, however, was not merely physical skill. Indeed, there is every indication that even with the best training methods that develop the highest levels of technical skill, we may not reach the heights of the truly great masters without concomitant training in the mental and philosophical disciplines of *budo* (martial ways).

So there is danger inherent in concentrating solely on the physical skills. It is equally important to approach karate-do from the standpoint of tradition, history, and the inherent values of the art to the cognitive and emotional facets of humankind. Each must complement the other.

Pure physical training will teach us very little about emotional stability or psychological well-being. The combined approach is, beyond a doubt, the best path to follow.

Karate is a weaponless means of self-defense, which consists of techniques of blocking or thwarting an attack and counter-attacking the opponent by punching, striking, or kicking.

The word itself literally means "empty hands." *Kara* means empty, and *te* means hands. Thus, karate is the art of "empty-hand fighting."

The progenitor of modern karate developed on Okinawa over several hundred years prior to the Meiji Restoration (1868), and was practiced in secret by the Okinawans, who were prohibited from possessing weapons. Until the 20th century, karate was mostly a disorganized conglomeration of various fighting techniques created by numerous Okinawans. Around the turn of the century, however, Gichin Funakoshi, an Okinawan schoolteacher who is now remembered as the father of modern karate, organized and systematized the art, blending together what he perceived to be the best elements created by the various practitioners.

Funakoshi, along with his two, primary teachers, Yoshitsune Itosu and Yoshitsune Azato, introduced karate into the Okinawan school system in 1903 as a physical education program, and in 1922, he formally introduced the art to Japan.

Karate proved to be so popular in Japan that by 1935, Funakoshi was able to propose that the art be called karate-do (pronounced as in "bread dough"), and be acknowledged as a formal Japanese art. In Japan, arts are thought of either in terms of technique (*jutsu*, as in ju-jutsu) or in terms of a way of life, or a path to follow for a correct and fulfilling life (*do*, as in judo).

Today, millions of people in virtually every country regularly practice karate-most of them pursuing the *do* aspects of the art.

In its modern manifestations, karate-do may be thought of as having three distinct aspects, viz., physical education, self-defense, and sport. But underlying each of these individually and all of them at once should be the inherent philosophy of the martial ways, viz., character, sincerity, effort, etiquette, and self-control.

The purpose of this book is to introduce students, beginners and advanced alike, to the traditional ideals and precepts of karate-do, and to suggest ways in which these ideals and precepts might be used to supplement their training.

Before we can grasp the essence of physical training, we must first endeavor to understand the philosophies and historical foundations upon which modern martial ways (*budo*) are built. Everyone who reads this book will have heard of karate, and most will have had some contact with it, if not personally, at least on television or in the movies.

What is disheartening to most dedicated practitioners is the fact that very few readers will have even a remote idea of the difference between karate-jutsu ("techniques of the empty hand"), and karate-do ("the way of life of the empty hand"), and the full-contact karate shown on television (which is not karate at all).

This book is primarily concerned with karate as a way of life (karate-do).

For people experienced in karate, it is important to study the traditional ideals of their art to better understand the nature of their art and to realize more intrinsic benefits from the pursuit of it. For people who have never entered a *dojo* (training hall), it is important to be familiar with the traditional ideals in order to exercise informed judgment when considering joining a *dojo*. It is not necessary, however, to be an expert in Japanese history or a great scholar to grasp the essence of where karate-do came from, why it has developed the way it has, or what we can expect from it in the future. All that is required is curiosity and an open mind.

1

From Japan to America: The Dilemmas of Change

Heraclitus said that there is nothing permanent except change, and Alfred North Whitehead said that "the art of progress is to preserve order amid change and to preserve change amid order." By Whitehead's standard, Japanese karate-do and the martial arts in general have failed, miserably, in the West. Many changes have occurred, but they inevitably have deteriorated into poor imitations of true karate-do. In America, in particular, the true martial arts have been commercialized—stripped naked, chopped to pieces, and hung out for lewd display in storefront "studios" from coast to coast. Most of these studios have closed for lack of interest and/or finances, but a few have flourished and grown large. It is, perhaps, a quintessential element of the American psyche to want to learn and master quickly, and then break away and become the Horatio Alger of the neighborhood. Indeed, a large slice of the American dream pie consists of the virtuous right to be independent, free from the domination of time clock and bosses. And the martial arts, with their commercially appealing, esoteric elements, have not been excepted from the lure of independent fame and fortune.

While most of the responsibility for the denigration of the arts must be placed squarely on the shoulders of enterprising Americans, some of it must also be borne by a few unscrupulous Japanese and Koreans who took money from American servicemen in exchange for a "bonafide" black belt certificate.

These GI's, in turn, brought their poorly learned arts home with them for further ruin by entrepreneurs. What all of this has led to in the United States is a state of chaos.

On one side of this many-faceted dilemma are the inelegant "moderns," who insist that the whole idea of keeping the martial arts traditional, and indeed Asian, is a gross waste of time. If you want to learn to fight and want to have more than 100 spectators at your tournament, they say, forget all about the traditional nonsense and do what works in America. On another side are the rigid "traditionalists," who insist that the martial arts be maintained in their original form. This group often speaks only Japanese in the *dojo* and seeks to imitate, in manner and in speech, the Japanese teachers with whom they have come into contact.

Another facet reflects traditionalists who have given up on the politics and economic problems, disassociated themselves from their instructors, and are practicing in their basements, their back yards and at local YMCAs and community centers. In many instances, the karate of these groups, while high in spirit, is low in technical proficiency. And, of course, there are the common citizens who wander into one school or another seeking physical improvement, self-defense, or the admiration of their peers. A less healthy atmosphere for the survival of true karate-do would be hard to imagine.

Nevertheless, true karate-do, as Gichin Funakoshi and his contemporaries taught it, is still alive and has a chance to survive, and even grow, if it can be peaceably and intelligently adapted to the American way of life. Adaptation is possible, but it requires a commitment of immense proportions.

The Japanese masters who introduced the art to America acknowledge the importance, necessity, and inevitability of adaptation and change, but not, perhaps, in the same manner to which Americans are accustomed. Hidetaka Nishiyama, the most famous rigid traditionalist leader in the karate world, and a direct pupil of Funakoshi, commented on this dilemma in an interview in 1978:

"I think any art changes day by day as people come up with better ideas for training and coaching techniques. I think the changes in training methods and more effective systems of training have been for the good, but I really don't see too many changes in the fundamental techniques we were practicing 15 or 20 years ago. Some people have indeed made changes of their own and even started their own systems and styles, but too often they have done this before they have completely digested every detail of their art. You see, it is very impertinent and foolish for a man with a few years of training to change techniques that have developed over several hundred years of research. If an individual has completely digested and internalized every aspect of his art, then and only then may he be qualified to change what he has learned. But these changes are few and far between.... In Japan, it was much easier to teach karate because all the people had the same cultural heritage and traditions, so it was not necessary to explain to them what they would gain from karate; they knew before they started training. Also, the Japanese, while they differ in size, do not differ significantly in the proportions of their body structures. That is, proportionately, almost all Japanese are the same. They are therefore able to imitate and pick up the movements of the instructor very easily. But in the United States, there are many different races and many diverse philosophical backgrounds. And the mixing of the races has produced wide-ranging body structures that are proportionately different from one another. It therefore became apparent... that we (the Japanese instructors) would have to coach more closely on the physical and scientific principles of body motion so that the Americans could adapt. To solve the problem, [we] undertook an intense study of kinesiology and body mechanics so that [we] would be able to better explain the underlying principles of physics and anatomy. My students could imitate my movements, but that would not make their movements correct or efficient. Simple imitation is no good. It is most important for the individual to feel the correct body action and understand it. The results of this type of

3

training may be that everyone looks different when performing the same technique. But how the technique looks is of no importance. What is important is that the student understand and apply the key points of each technique from the principles of dynamics, kinesiology, and so on. Americans are more difficult to teach than the Japanese, but mostly because [they] must be taught the philosophy of karate, the underlying philosophy of the martial arts. If they do not learn this, they will look good on the outside, but will miss the main point of karate, which lies in the development of the human self. The Japanese already understand the philosophy, if not in words and developed concepts, certainly in feeling and in spirit."

"To make matters worse, non-Japanese people often gain a superficial understanding of the philosophy and think they have it. But in reality they do not have the inner feeling that flows from the human spirit. Imparting these concepts and feelings to the non-Japanese is our challenge.

"I think America has the best chance for the advanced development of karate, because it is a new nation without a unified cultural heritage of long standing or a uniform philosophy of life. This makes Americans eager to seek out the depths of Oriental philosophy, and many of them have already established a strong base in this regard. I think many European countries have a very strong cultural heritage, and by and large, they are not seeking a new philosophy, nor are they receptive to it. In this regard, I think the Americans have a big advantage."[1]

Permeating Nishiyama's words is the over-riding sense that karate-do (as he perceives it) is something much more than the mastery of physical techniques. "How the technique looks is of no importance," he says, and warns that a superficial understanding of karate-do will lead the student away from "the inner feeling that flows from the human spirit." If this seems unclear, it is because Nishiyama faces the problem that all the Japanese masters must face: it is impossible to explain and ingrain in a few words the principles of a culture that has developed steadily over several thousand years. Even Gichin

Funakoshi himself is of little help in this regard. In *Karate-do Kyohan,* he writes, "True karate-do is this: that in daily life, one's mind and body be trained and developed in a spirit of humility; and that in critical times, one be devoted utterly to the cause of justice."[2] While simple in translation, his definition in Japanese imparts far more to the Japanese reader than can be perceived in English. To more clearly understand what Nishiyama and Funakoshi are taking for granted, one must have some understanding of the history and psychological make-up of the Japanese people, of Japanese combat, of the samurai code of honor, *bushido,* and of how modern *budo* (martial ways) developed from these influences. The intrinsic principles of modern Japanese karate-do, and indeed the principles of all Japanese *budo,* derive directly from the traditions of the Japanese feudal warriors. These fierce, armor-clad, professional warriors were called *bushi,* and their arts were known as *bugei* ("martial arts"). During the Muromachi period of Japanese history (1392–1573), the *bushi* were more often called samurai, and it is this term that is now commonly used to describe these heroic fighters. "Samurai" is a derivative of a word that means "to be at one's side," and more properly reflects the nature of the *bushi* in service to a lord.

The rise of the *bushi* in Japan commenced with the rise of the Fujiwara clan in the ninth century. For reasons of expedience, the Fujiwaras delegated responsibility for various military affairs to the Taira and Minamoto clans. As the Fujiwaras grew weaker, the Taira and Minamoto groups gradually usurped power and authority until the military ultimately ruled the country. With the onset of military rule and strict adherence to feudalistic principles, the professional *bushi* was imbued with both power and responsibilities that far exceeded the rights of the common man.

Since they were at the top of the social structure, the *bushi* gradually developed a code of conduct and responsibility which later became known as *bushido,* "the way of the warrior." *Bushido* was a natural outgrowth of the high position of the

5

bushi in society, and was strongly and directly influenced by Confucian, Shinto, Buddhist, and Chinese societal precepts. What began as *kyuba no michi* ("the way of the bow and the horse") in the 12th century, developed into *bushido* by the 17th century, and can be defined as consisting of seven broad principles: commitment to justice, courage, benevolence, courtesy, honesty, personal honor and loyalty to superiors.

Clearly, *bushido* owes its birth to the fact that Japan was a society with half a million warriors occupying the upper strata, but who had no wars to fight. It thus became imperative to them that they maintain their position of respect and dignity by formalizing the arts of war. Those who had formerly perfected the arts of war for killing now turned to the perfection of the arts for the perfection of character. Those who did not look deeply into themselves and seek this perfection of character were often cut loose from the employ of their lords and became mercenaries. Known as *ronin* ("wave men"), these disenfranchised samurai roamed the land looking for any kind of vio-

lence that would offer pay. But by and large, most *bushi* turned their energies toward self-cultivation under the code of *bushido* during the peaceful Tokugawa period.

When battles did occur, they were not at all like modern warfare. The samurai, after all, were important people in society who paid no taxes and existed solely for the protection and propagation of their individual lords. A battle between samurai typically consisted of two lines of warriors facing each other, and leaders strutting forward to recite their battle poem or extol their own virtues. After telling each other how great and fearsome they were, the two leaders would sometimes fight to the death, ending the battle before it began. More often, however, the fighting began as soon as (but definitely not before) the formal speeches ended, with the samurai attacking each other in hundreds or thousands of individual battles, man to man, sword to sword. It was the type of warfare upon which individual legends are readily built, and the victorious samurai would almost always discuss and record the artistic and aesthetic values of the battle for future generations.

Under the code of *bushido*, commitment to justice and courage were precepts ingrained in the samurai from birth. While killing under the direction of or in defense of one's lord was justified, simply killing for the sake of killing was not. Under the influence of Zen, courage became a matter of serenity and composure—not merely physical disregard of fear. Many stories of feudal combat end with the dying samurai composing his death poem while the blood flows from his body, thus showing his presence of mind and courage. This was also afforded much respect by the victor, who would politely pause while his conquered foe died with dignity; he would then usually cut off the dead man's head and parade around with it on the end of a spear to accept the honor and awe associated with his victory over such a great *bushi*.

Benevolence was known as *bushi no nasake* ("tenderness of a warrior"), and characterized the formal attitude of the samurai toward all the lower classes. In this sense, benevolence

meant that while a samurai might kill someone who offended his lord, he might not kill the man's family. Clearly, the benevolence of the *bushi* could not be mistaken for weakness or uncertainty.

The courtesy of the samurai was a product of self-discipline, superiority, and loyalty. To act in an impolite manner at any time was to indicate a lack of these three qualities. And without self-discipline, superiority of physical and mental powers, and loyalty to one's lord, one could not be a true samurai.

For the *bushi*, honesty was not merely a matter of always telling the truth. It was a matter so intrinsically interwoven with the other principles of *bushido* that the warrior actually treated lying as a terminal disease. Lying would cause a terrible death, he believed, and the rest of his society acknowledged his veracity by calling it *bushi no ichi-gon*, which meant that the word of a *bushi* was inviolate and incorruptible. When a *bushi* gave his word, no written contract was necessary.

The *bushi's* sense of personal honor undoubtedly played a role in developing trust in his honesty, also: a *bushi* whose honor was questioned or offended would instantly cut down the offending scoundrel who would be so bold as to call his truthfulness into question.

The last, and perhaps most pervasive, trait of the samurai was his loyalty to his master. It was this loyalty that granted him his position in society, and indeed his right to exist as a *bushi*. Such loyalty was unflagging in the extreme. If the *bushi* preferred death to dishonor, it was because any dishonor to him, personally, reflected on the honor of his master. And the "master" could be a just cause or a field leader as well as a lord.

As a formal, workable code to be used in daily life, *bushido* was, and in large measure still is, a fundamental precept of Japanese life. Its tenets are not limited to the warrior, but extend to familial relations, business dealings, and virtually all student-teacher relationships.

It is to this code that Gichin Funakoshi is speaking when he describes karate-do in terms of humility, justice, dedication, loyalty to the *sensei*, and so on. And it is from this tradition that modern karate-do arose. The formality of combat lies at the very roots of Japanese thinking and culture, and virtually all arts that purport to be a *Do* ("way" or "path") share a consanguineous relationship with the samurai and *bushido*.

To paraphrase Daidoji Yuzan, who wrote *Budo Shoshin Shu* in the 18th century, the major precepts of *bushido* for the samurai were as follows:

1. The essence of true courage lies in living when it is time to live and dying when it is time to die.

2. Truthfulness is a matter of life and death. The code of *bushido* demands that a samurai carefully consider every word before uttering it, and that his words be true. Anything less than truth results in a bad death.

3. Moderation in everything is a virtue.

4. The idea of death should be kept in the front of the mind at all times—whether working, eating, or sleeping.

5. True virtue is like a tree with branches. The samurai is a branch, and his lord is the trunk.

6. As the samurai is the branch of the tree, so are his parents also the trunk.

7. The samurai will be faithful to his lord no matter what circumstances arise. He will fight to the death for his lord, even if he is the last soldier to face 10,000 enemies.

8. To prove his loyalty, the samurai will walk boldly into the flying arrows of the enemy, welcoming death.

9. The three primary, in-bred virtues of the true samurai are loyalty to one's lord, commitment to justice, and courage.

10. As a sign of his proper position and that of his lord, a samurai will never point his feet in the direction of his lord's quarters when sleeping, nor will he allow his arrows or spear to be pointed in that direction.

11. A samurai must always rise when he hears his lord's name and when he speaks of his lord himself.

12. A samurai will die in the face of the enemy with a smile on his face.

13. A samurai will appear to be full and languid, even if he is starving.

14. If mortally wounded, the samurai will, nevertheless, remain composed, and he will still exercise the proper respect for his superiors.

15. Strength, by itself, is no virtue. The samurai must also be a master of science, poetry, and tea ceremony.

With these basic concepts in mind, it is much easier to grasp the essence of how Gichin Funakoshi perceived his fledgling art, but such knowledge, by itself, is of little help in bridging the gap between tradition and modern application.

If we are to find a workable manner in which to adapt the traditional *bushido* concepts of karate-do to modern life (or, perhaps, adapt ourselves to the traditional concepts), we must first clearly define the essence of karate-do, enumerate and elucidate its tenets and benefits for modern people, and delineate the aesthetic, moral, and practical guidelines by which it might function in daily life.

In the physical sense, karate is fairly easy to recognize. It is a self-defensive art that consists of techniques of blocking, punching, striking, and kicking. In order for it to be, in the classical Japanese sense, true karate, its techniques must be performed with *kime* (focus). *Kime* is far more than the mere tensing of body muscles, although it has been mistaken for this by almost all who have formed their own modern styles. Indeed, *kime* has both physical and psychological correlates, which must be brought together in a coordinated effort at the completion of each technique. The techniques of karate must also be practiced in a series of formal exercises (*kata*), which contain all the essential elements of self-defense, body shifting, changing positions, and so on. These *kata* are handed down from the masters of years past, and while they may be modified somewhat by the new masters, they are never blatantly changed, nor are new *kata* created. Among karate masters, the physical aspects described above are pretty much taken for granted. There is virtually no disagreement on what constitutes the physical description of karate. Regardless of the style of technique, so long as it displays punching, striking, kicking, blocking, *kime*, and *kata*, it can reasonably be defined as karate.

Beyond this most general and vague definition lies the essence of karate-do, or karate as a way of life. Herein lies the greatest controversy, confusion, bitter rivalries, and chaos.

Without exception, the Japanese karate masters insist that karate-do is pure *budo*. That is, it is drawn from the tradition of Japanese *budo* and conforms, in spirit and essence, to all the traditional precepts of *budo* and *bushido*. Modern Shotokan karate-do is certainly close to traditional *budo* in its outward appearance. It seeks strong, individual techniques; it is highly disciplined, both physically and mentally; it purports to develop character, sincerity, effort, etiquette and self-control; and it encourages the development of and adherence to the traditional precepts and tenets of classical *budo*. But modern Shotokan karate-do faces two dilemmas that are not readily solved.

First, a particular dilemma for the Japanese is that karate-do, while conforming in spirit and essence to the traditional precepts and tenets of *bushido*, has no direct link to traditional

Japanese *budo*. That is, for a modern *budo* to be fully and unquestionably defined as *budo*, it must derive directly from one or more of the forms of traditional *bujutsu*. Kendo, for example, came from ken-jutsu, kyudo from kyu-jutsu, iaido from iai-jutsu, and so on. Karate-do, however, along with arts like judo and aikido, is a modern *shin budo*, a *do* derived from the principles of the classical *bujutsu*, but not a direct descendant in the blood sense. The modern derivations bear a blood relationship to the classical *bujutsu*, but they are, in reality, half-brothers.

The second dilemma is faced by both Japanese and Westerners. It is that there is not yet enough flexibility on either side to successfully bridge the large gap in thinking and attitude between East and West. It seems clear that some modern masters like the late Masatoshi Nakayama, first Chief Instructor of the Japan Karate Association, have made an effort to bridge the gap, at least partially, in the form of scientific and rational analysis of body mechanics, physiology, kinesiology, psychology and the like, but the effect has been minuscule on the overall problem. Indeed, many Americans find great difficulty in following the scientific path prescribed by Nakayama and others, because it invariably leads them (the Americans) to scientific discoveries of their own, which, when presented to the Japanese, are rejected or ignored. And they are ignored, more often than not, because the Japanese masters, by and large, still consider it impertinent for Americans to question the Japanese traditions—including those "traditions" which have only come about in the last 20 or 30 years. This latter dilemma is particularly problematic, because it seems to rational Americans that the Japanese are inflexible, condescending and egocentric. It is very difficult, and perhaps impossible, to rationally and scientifically analyze tradition—particularly when the Japanese will choose tradition over science every time.

There is absolutely nothing the West can do to solve the first dilemma, and, in a very real sense, it is a problem that matters only to the Japanese. The second dilemma, however, is very real and important to the West, and its solution is critical to the survival and transmission of true karate-do for future generations. In order to grasp the delicate nature of this dilemma, it is necessary to look back in Japanese history and attempt to

perceive the elements of Japanese culture and family life that manifest themselves in the *dojo*. It is not necessary to go back very far.

The Japanese feudal system brought two great precepts to modern Japan, which bear directly and heavily on the development of karate-do and related arts. The first of these is the intrinsic value of the superiority of the human spirit over materialism. On the surface, this seems simple, but when taken as an intrinsic value of Japanese life and thinking, it necessarily becomes paramount in any discussion of East versus West.

When the Japanese entered World War II, for example, they clearly knew that the American forces, in particular, would be larger in numbers, better equipped, better organized, and tactically superior. But even with this knowledge, the Japanese honestly believed they would prevail because they had the spirit to prevail. Their spirit was culturally pervasive and unified. It was, from Emperor to peasant, the strongest force in the land. And it seemed clear to them that America had no similar spirit. The emphasis in America was on bigness—the bigger and more technologically superior, the better. In Japan, there was no virtue at all in bigness or technological superiority; their fundamental approach to everything was based on the spirit of man overcoming the evil machinery. As Noel Perrin has pointed out in *Giving Up the Gun*, the Japanese are the only society in history that voluntarily gave up firearms and reverted to swords because the sword was more aesthetically pleasing and closer to the true spirit of the individual man. Guns also endangered the tradition of the samurai generals' battle speeches and poems: the other side would just shoot the man as he talked. But taken alone, the high value of spirit over materialism is not sufficient to fully describe nor analyze the dilemma now faced by Americans seeking to understand karate-do. What is far more important is the Japanese idea of hierarchy, or "proper station." This concept, more than any other, is at the root of the division between the thinking of East and West, and it is permeated with the notion of the superiority of spirit over materialism.

Class Structure of Feudal Japan

Military Class
(*buke*)
Central Government
(*bakufu*)
Provincial Government
(*daimyo*)

Imperial Court and Nobles
(*kuge*)

Religious Orders

Commoners
(*heimin*)
Farmers
(*hyakusho*)
Artisans
(*shokunin*)
Merchants
(*akindo, chonin*)
Outcasts
(*eta, hinin*)

The rise of the warrior class, it must be remembered, gave impetus to and ultimately solidified the Japanese feudal system. At the top of the structure was the military class (*buke*), which included the central government (*bakufu*) and the provincial government (*daimyo*). It also must be remembered that the warriors had no wars to fight for over 200 years. A step down from the warriors were the commoners (*heimin*), which consisted of the farmers (*hyakusho*), followed by the artisans (*shokumin*), the merchants (*akindo* or *chonin*), and the out-

15

casts (*eta* or *hinin*). Between the military class and the commoners were the Imperial Court and nobles (*kuge*). From the 12th through the 19th centuries, the Japanese were born, lived, and died under this rigid hierarchical system, and they lived under it successfully and happily. In large measure, they were successful and happy because their concept of hierarchy was not at all like the feudal hierarchy of Europe, nor was it akin to the American concept of authoritarianism. Indeed, the Japanese concept of feudalism is diametrically opposed, in spirit, essence, and execution, to the West's concept of vassals, lords, and peasants.

In each stratum of Japanese feudal society there was imbued an almost equal amount of responsibility with rights. That is, while the samurai were the guardians of the dignity of their class and that of their lords, they were at the same time required to be sincere, honest, courteous, righteous in the extreme, and properly responsive to the actions and attitudes of the lower classes. Japanese feudalism was a reciprocal arrangement. The farmers, for example, were the backbone of the society. They provided food for the other classes, and taxes on farmers at the height of Japanese feudalism amounted to almost 50 percent. This, by European standards (under 10 percent), would have been outrageous. At the same time, however, farmers were granted land to farm in perpetuity, and their complaints had a special priority on the agendas of the courts. It was not (as it often was in Europe) a hardship to be a farmer in feudal Japan; indeed it was a good position with many benefits, and it was a position of respect. At the lower end of the spectrum, the merchants bore the brunt of most of the negative feelings of the upper classes, but even they were not summarily executed for transgressions (except in the case of those who did not show proper respect to a samurai or his lord). Merchants are always a problem in a rigid feudal system, because it is they who have the most opportunity to make more money and buy influence. In Japan, merchants who grew too large or became too prosperous were forced to invest their money in projects ordered by the government. In this manner, the balance of wealth was maintained without anyone suffering unduly. The entire system functioned so well, in fact, that there were very few Japanese who could be considered outcasts. The outcasts were usually beggars, poor con artists, skinners, and tanners, and frequently were assigned such tasks as cleaning up after a samurai who tested his blade on the body of a prisoner, and disposing of the body.

Through much of its feudal era, Japan was at peace, and as has already been noted, the warrior class turned to the perfection of skills for the perfection of character. They became authorities on flower arranging, tea ceremony, and poetry, and these arts became, naturally, abilities held in high esteem and regard by the other classes.

But more importantly, and perhaps more directly to the point, family life and personal relationships became directly and forcefully imbued with the feudal concepts of "proper station" or "proper position." Since the whole system was a reciprocal arrangement between upper and lower classes, it was relatively easy and natural for intricate formalities to develop between them. The more formal and the more intricate, the better. Also, intricate formality left less room for inadvertent offensive action. In both speech and gesture, the Japanese developed distinctly different words and actions to be used for different members of society. The act of bowing, for example, has much more significance for the Japanese than for Westerners who view it without the benefit of Japanese cultural heritage. There are many ways to bow, depending on one's station in society, to whom one is bowing, whether one is initiating the bow or returning it, and so on. A farmer's bow to a samurai, for example, would be long and low, similar to a samurai's bow to his lord. And the samurai might be required to respond with only a nod of the head or a slight bow from the shoulders; the lord might not have to acknowledge the bow at all. Even today, two people training in karate, for example, may not bow to one another at all in daily life, but if one is senior to the other in

karate training, they will use the formal bowing procedures required of the relationship when they are in the *dojo*. And this system is sacrosanct; even the worst enemies outside the *dojo* will readily adhere to the formality required inside the *dojo*. And they will do it without considering their personal relationship; it is morally and socially required.

One's proper station is not merely one's position in society, but in the natural order of the universe as well. It is also one's position in one's family. Filial piety is a concept of great strength in Japan, and families are formally structured according to generation, sex, and age. While the father is generally the head of the household, the family structure extends to the grandparents also. As noted, the hierarchy of the family is determined first by generation, second by sex (males always have the superior position), and third by age. And the formal methods of bowing that are seen on the street and in companies are used just as vigorously in the family living room. The children always bow to their elders, the wife always bows to her husband, and the husband will always bow to his father or older brother. Further, this is not merely a matter of outward formality. Until he formally retires, the father and/or grandfather will actually pass judgment on the activities and dealings of the younger sons. The duty of making decisions and giving valuable advice is then passed to the eldest son. So deeply ingrained is this system in the Japanese way of life, that a Japanese who wishes to express total confusion or utter bewilderment will say, literally, that the problem is "neither elder brother nor younger brother." This is equivalent to the English phrases "black and white" or "as different as night and day." It implies that two things or concepts are clearly distinguishable beyond any reasonable doubt. Black is black and white is white; older brother is older brother, and younger brother is younger brother. Within the family unit, the older brother always makes decisions for the younger brother and enforces these decisions with perfect moral rectitude and without much discussion or consideration of the younger brother's feelings or point of view.

Of course, in traditional Japanese families, the younger brother would not think of expressing feelings or a point of view contrary to the decisions of his elder brother. It would be unthinkable. Again, it is important to distinguish between this seemingly authoritarian structure and the Western concept of authoritarianism. In the West, such despotic power over another human being is subject to strict social sanction. In Japan, however, we must bear in mind that the older brother has not only power over the younger brother, but also vast and detailed responsibilities for the care and upbringing of the

young ones. It is, like most aspects of the Japanese feudal system, a reciprocal arrangement.

With this basic information about Japanese thinking and family life, we can examine the actions of the Japanese karate masters from a more informed stance, and perhaps we can draw some enlightening conclusions about the nature and philosophy of Japanese karate-do as Gichin Funakoshi and his immediate successors have perceived it.

First, karate-do was brought to life in Japan less than 20 years before World War II—a time of great national unification for the Japanese. It was also the last period in Japanese history wherein the Japanese as a whole were actively seeking to broaden their physical empire in the world—to create the proper world order, they called it, with each country in its "proper station." Japan, of course, would be at the top of this structure. Throughout the 1920s and 1930s, Japan dedicated itself to the development of industry and technology that would be used to win the war, but at the same time impressed upon her people the most important weapon of all: the supreme Japanese spirit.

The attitude of the Japanese soldiers was not overlooked by the Americans they fought. Much to the chagrin and, indeed, disgust, of the Americans, the Japanese troops fought in a manner that reflected their national spirit. Death, they believed, was itself a victory of the spirit. Anything less than an all-out struggle of life and death, regardless of the odds or the outcome, they believed, was not worthy of praise. They simply could not understand why Western troops would surrender. Nor could they comprehend why the Americans had medical corps to tend to the wounded. When the Japanese were hospitalized and the enemy was advancing, requiring an evacuation of the hospital, those who could not be moved would be shot by the doctors or would be allowed to commit suicide. In an all-out struggle, you see, only victory or death are acceptable outcomes. And, contrary to the beliefs of many Americans, the Japanese were not indoctrinated with these ideas just to go into combat. Indeed, death before dishonor was deeply ingrained in the sinews and bones of their society. No one had to tell them; it had been instilled in them from the day they were born. Suicide was also a way of spitting in the technological eye of America: "Your guns and machines may be important to you, but they can't take me; only I can take me, and would rather do that than surrender my spirit to your material barbarism."

This gives us some insight into the words of Gichin Funakoshi when he talks of karate in terms of "seeds of destruction" that "lurk deep within the shadows of human culture." And we can also understand a little more clearly why he would speak of "History [as] the story of the rise and fall of nations" in the preface of a karate book. He warns of complacency in the Japanese spirit, and encourages the study of karate for the renewal and perpetuation of the character and fiber of Japanese life. Clearly, he intended for karate-do to be practiced in the spirit of traditional Japanese concepts—both those concepts arising generally from feudalism and those specific concepts that form the foundation of *bushido*.

Second, throughout Funakoshi's writings there is drawn the picture of a man who stresses humility, subjugation of one's self to one's superiors, and all the samurai traditions of justice, courage, sincerity, veracity, honor, and so on. This is how Gichin Funakoshi and the Japanese people in general perceived their world, and it is these concepts that he stressed when teaching his students.

At this point, several important points come more clearly into focus.

First, the Japanese who began spreading karate around the world in the late 1950s and early 1960s are products of the culture in which they were raised. They believe strongly in the virtue, indeed in the necessity, of a rigid hierarchy, and they find the Western (especially the American) attachment to equality in all things as curious and suspicious. Their whole lives, including every nuance of their family lives, have been structured along strict hierarchical lines, and it must certainly be a shock to enter a culture where everything is in direct opposition to what they have been taught and believe. To them, it must be "neither older brother nor younger brother."

Second, Americans may see something as apparently simple as a bow as a shameful action, or at best, a silly waste of time. So Americans bow to appease the Japanese teachers, and the teachers know the bow is not sincere. And how does one tell another that he should show more respect, should use a different form of language for the *sensei* (teacher), the *sempai* (seniors) and the *kohai* (juniors)? Clearly, it is a difficult problem.

Finally, what the Japanese intuitively feel as aesthetically pleasing and beautiful, Americans tend to view as superfluous. Among the "moderns" in karate, we often hear the complaint that what the Japanese insist on (bowing, *kata*, rigid formality)

is absolutely useless in developing fighting skill. The Japanese answer to this might be that karate-do has nothing to do with just developing fighting skill—a rejoinder hardly likely to bring droves of macho Americans into the *dojo*.

A conclusion to be drawn from the dilemmas of change is that karate-do undoubtedly has great value for the Japanese, but that such values may not be valid for most Americans. For Americans to truly perceive the same aesthetically pleasing qualities the Japanese perceive in their art, they necessarily would have to become Japanese. On the other hand, for the Japanese karate masters to become American enough in their thinking to communicate properly with Americans, their whole lives would have to be started anew. They would have to live in an American household as a baby and spend the next 20 or 30 years re-learning a completely different way of life. Neither alternative is viable.

What must be done is for Americans and other Westerners to rise as high as possible in karate-do and then delineate the values the art might bear for modern Western life. If they will study hard and try to rise as high as the Japanese masters—both physically and philosophically—a truly Western aesthetic of the art might someday be given birth, attended by midwives from both East and West.

2

The Sun Source

While modern karate-do is usually described purely in terms of Japanese thought, it is essential to acknowledge the older Chinese thinking and philosophy as the sun source of all the martial ways. Indeed, if we are to seek a new, truly Western aesthetic of karate-do, we must first consider all the major influences—both metaphysical and philosophical—that have converged over the last several thousand years to form the heart and mind of *budo*, *bushido*, and, consequently, karate-do itself.

A large part of Japanese philosophical thought is derived, more or less directly, from ancient Chinese thought, and while the symbols may have changed, the essential elements have not. That is, the concept of dualism that permeates Chinese thought also permeates Japanese thinking. In order to scrutinize this fundamental element of Eastern thought for the purpose of integrating it into Western thinking, we must first have a basic understanding of how it originally developed.

Chinese philosophy from the late Chou period (about 500–222 B.C.) was, from its inception, a system whose foundation was composed of opposite, but complementary, aspects. The Chinese have always shown equal concern for both the philosophical and practical sides of life. Their beliefs are rooted in the notion that one cannot function successfully in society or government or personal relationships without both practical guidelines for action and philosophical notions of how actions reflect and are reflected in nature.

The Chinese sages, moreover, displayed a propensity for expounding their metaphysical and religious ideals in the con-

crete terms of the merchant, the farmer, and the soldier. They were very pragmatic in their view that the common man has neither the inclination nor the capability to throw down his tools and enter monastic life to transcend to a higher plane of consciousness.

Further, the average citizen, whether today or 2,000 years ago, often has no clear image of specifically what is bothering him. The stresses and dissatisfactions of daily life, while rendering obvious results in the form of tension and anxiety, are themselves vague, abstract feelings and ideas that lurk beneath the surface of the moonlit pond of the mind.

Western prescriptions for peace of mind, self-realization, and actualization of a calm and steady demeanor typically treat the symptom while ignoring the disease. That is, much of Western psychology and, for the most part, Western religions, tend to treat the obvious results (the symptoms) of the anxiety, while largely ignoring the relationship of the human organism to its environment and to nature itself. Moreover, the Western patient would be hard put to "find the motion in stillness and the stillness in motion" prescribed by Gichin Funakoshi and ancient philosophers.

A symbol used to study this phenomenon is called, in Chinese, *yin-yang*, and it is, according to Chinese tradition, the ultimate and enduring symbol of the nature of the universe and all actions and forces. In the West, it is frequently used as a symbol of importance by practitioners of Korean fighting arts, Chinese tai chi and various meditative sects.

The *yin-yang* is, on the surface, a visual representation of the dualistic nature of all things. The darker side with the white dot is *yin*, and it represents negative, receptive and passive. The corresponding white half with the black dot is *yang*, and it represents positive, active and aggressive.

The *yin-yang* symbol is a clear representation of not only Chinese thinking, but of Eastern thought in general. Whatever the problem, whatever the question under consideration, the truth may be represented by this symbol. It is a clear represen-

tation of the duality of all things, all thoughts, all people. For the positive to be realized (*yang*), the negative (*yin*) must be manifest. One defines the other, and in each there lurks the seed of the other.

Thus, in the negative blackness of *yin*, there is the positive whiteness of *yang*, and vice versa. And the symbol is not a static drawing on a piece of paper; it is a dynamic, spinning sphere. As truth itself is never static, the *yin-yang* is always in motion, with the negative drawing power and force from the positive, itself becoming positive. And the positive always gives freely to the negative, never becoming fixed for a measurable instant.

It is through this ebb and flow of positive and negative forces, in the constant flux between active and passive, that the truth resides, no matter what the subject.

Of the many facets of Chinese thought and philosophy, two clearly stand out as the most significant and influential. These two are Confucianism and Taoism.

Confucianism is the heritage of Confucius, a great scholar and teacher who emphasized the value of learning from cul-

tural heritage and transcending the mundane aspects of daily life in search of perfection of the human character. The emphasis in Confucianism is on practical matters of day-to-day life, the structuring of society, and the acquisition of knowledge in a functional sense. Both Chinese rules of etiquette and education are drawn from Confucianism, and the practice of ancestor veneration and worship is a product of Confucian thinking.

Taoism, on the other hand, is derived primarily from the teaching of the sage, Lao Tzu, who is purported to be the author of the *Tao Te Ching*. Unlike the Six Classics of Confucian tradition (which detailed laws, rules, rituals, and the like), the *Tao Te Ching* is a series of 81 poetic aphorisms stressing the paradoxical nature of human existence and the unity of man and nature. While the Confucian Classics are histories written in a style permitting very little deviant interpretation, the *Tao Te Ching* is written in characters which, like poetry and impressionistic drawings, suggest various meanings and are subject to myriad interpretations. Not surprisingly, there are as many translations of the *Tao Te Ching* as there are translators who have approached the task. The *Tao Te Ching*, along with the *Chuang-tzu*, comprises the most influential paradigm of Chinese thought as it relates to the importance of following the laws of nature and merging with the ebb and flow of nature in the quest for human insight and happiness. The influences of Confucianism, Taoism, and Chan Buddhism comprises the foundation of Chinese thought, philosophy, metaphysics, and actions. It is from these sources that the Chinese have come to believe that there is a unifying force in the universe that underlies, gives coherence to, and oversees all that is before us. This force they call the *Tao*.

The Chinese view the *Tao* as the essence of all the universe, the ultimate reality—unlimited by doctrine, thought, or action. As such, it can be represented by the *yin-yang* symbol, because it is constantly in a state of motion and change. What the Japanese martial artists call shu-ha-ri to describe the cyclical nature of the universe, the Chinese call *yin-yang*, and they believe that if people go too far in either direction, they ultimately will come back to where they started. That is, if we pursue wealth to its ultimate ends, we will find poverty; and in poverty there can be true wealth. The seeds of the one are always found in the other. As male and female and dark and light exist at once in opposition and complementary to one another, so do the forces of the universe ebb and flow throughout nature. Had we been there 5,000 years ago, we might have seen Chinese scholars deducing all of this as they recorded the comings and goings of the sun and moon, the rise and fall of crops, and the cycle of the seasons. These are the true laws, they believed, and while immutable, they are irregular in their specific rate of change. That is, they are in a constant state of flux. The deduction became clear: the essence of a correct and fulfilling life is to live in harmony with the *Tao*—to harmoniously proceed within the dynamic *Tao*, avoiding conflicts with nature along the way.

Since the *yin-yang* symbol represents the *Tao* itself, it can be thought of as representing anything and everything. Indeed, *yin* and *yang* were studied closely by the Chinese and were represented hexagramatically in the *I Ching* or Book of Changes. The *I Ching* is the first of the six Confucian Classics, and its hexagrams represent all the possible combinations of *yin* and *yang* in broken (*yin*) and unbroken (*yang*) lines. These hexagrams have been used by the Chinese for centuries to divine the meaning of life, the nature of individual phenomena, and the correct actions to take in any given situation. The hexagrams are "pictures of the concepts," and they represent the patterns of the *Tao* itself.

Throughout the centuries, untold thousands of volumes have been written regarding the nature of *yin* and *yang*, but for one to use the *yin-yang* symbol as a key to understanding the philosophical foundations of karate-do, one only needs to know some basics. From the viewpoint of martial arts, the most important interpretations are as follows:

Qualities of Yin and Yang

Yin	*Yang*
Dark	Light
Female	Male
Intuitive	Rational
Negative	Positive
Passive	Aggressive
Receptive	Active
Contemplative	Creative
Cold	Hot
Body Surface	Internal Body

What is most important to bear in mind is that the *yin-yang* symbol itself is never static; it is always in motion.

And while the polarity between dark and light, cold and hot, and so on, is distinct at the extremes of each pole, the distinctions are not so clear in the areas between. Lukewarm water, for example, is neither distinctly hot nor cold. It is somewhere in between. And no human being is completely black or completely white; we each display varying shades somewhere in between. Thus, the polarity of *yin-yang* is not the ultimate truth nor guide for life: it is precisely the lack of absolute polarity which forces us to respond spontaneously in any given situation and find the truth. Whether in matters of business, personal relationships, or physical exercise, the truth as we perceive it is somewhere in between the distinct poles.

The illustration serves to illuminate the course of the spinning *yin-yang*. Starting at point A, the dark *yin* is at its smallest, and grows progressively larger as the course around the circle is followed. At point B, the dark *yin* is completely dominant, at which point it gradually turns into light *yang*. And it is important to note that the change is gradual, just as night and day do not begin and end with distinct demarcations. Dark gradually gives way to light, and light gradually fades to dark. And this is not to suggest that life is simply a spinning circle in

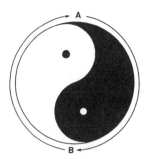

which we are trapped. Indeed, the *yin-yang* spins continuously along the path of time. The following illustration more accurately reflects the course of the *yin-yang* in relation to time.

This also illustrates the idea that the *yin-yang* is a representation of the *Tao*, and that the forces of the *Tao* are as much inside us as outside. At any point on the line of life shown above, the forces of *yin* and *yang* are in motion, balancing and counter-balancing each other. According to Asian thought, it is when we allow these forces to become unbalanced that we become ill, weak, fatigued and anxious.

To consider it in another light, consider that the Western view of life, death, and humanity in general is linear, while the Eastern view of the life-death phenomena is cyclical.

Western science believes that humanity had dark, obscure beginnings, and that it progressed and is progressing toward a bright goal that will lead either to ideal existence or ultimate catastrophe. The Eastern view, on the other hand, is that the past was very bright, the present is somewhat darker, and the future is very bright indeed.

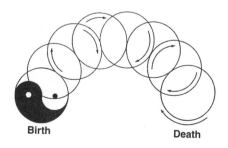

Birth   **Death**

From a religious perspective, the points of view may be contrasted as follows:

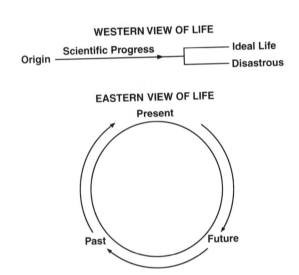

Regardless of the point of view one chooses, it is clear that the cyclical Eastern view stands in stark contrast to the Western linear view.

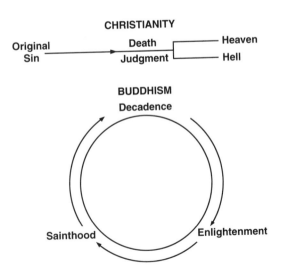

What this thinking has brought to the martial ways and Buddhism and Eastern life in general is the supreme virtue of developing the "spontaneous mind," which reacts to each situation instinctively, intuitively, and without fear or looking back. Once the truth is perceived, and once the ultimate opposing poles are understood, the spontaneous mind may follow the natural course of life and death. That is, it may follow the natural flow of the universe—whether we call that flow *Tao, satori, mushin, Do,* or the Holy Spirit. Both Taoists and Zen masters strive for the same thing: to realize one's own true nature and the nature of the universe, and to flow spontaneously from one's intuition in accord with the laws of nature. In all matters and actions, we must proceed from the truth that "in form there is emptiness and in emptiness there is form." Indeed, according to the Buddhist *Hannya Shingyo* sutra, in the phrase Gichin Funakoshi used to create the word "karate," "form itself is emptiness, and emptiness itself is form." What this means is that we must cut away all preconceived ideas and notions of reality, form, matter, and existence, and appreciate each thing and each moment exactly as it is. A statue, for example, is "form," but came from formless material. In the formless clay or bronze or iron there was in fact form (the statue), which was merely realized by a particular artist. When the statue is melted down, the form again returns to formlessness, and throughout the entire process, the fundamental nature of the materials has not changed: clay is still clay, and bronze is still bronze. As the statue is a representation of a thought or idea or concept or "thing," so are our preconceived notions about reality merely illusions superimposed on the fundamental nature of reality.

The first precept of the spirit of *budo* is to see and accept things as they really are, without superimposing our own interpretations on them. Death, which we have so long believed to be bad, can in fact be perceived as something entirely natural and, therefore, good. What if, for example, death is not nearly so bad as our perception of it? What if death is merely the

changing of form into formlessness or formlessness into form? Would it not be a good thing to know that all energy, including our own individual life force, is already and eternally existing, and cannot be either created or destroyed? If we are already eternal, why should we worry about our illusion of death as an ending? Of course, there are not satisfactory rational answers to these questions. And that is exactly where Eastern philosophy and mysticism leaves us: there are no answers because ultimately there are no questions. In our search for a truly Western aesthetic of karate-do, this is where we must start: there are no answers. We shall have to wait and see if there are indeed questions.

Beyond the general metaphysical and philosophical influences of Chinese thinking on the development of *budo*, there are some readily ascertainable, specific influences that have contributed to the development of modern karate-do. The oldest written records indicate that the Chinese have long practiced various breathing and flexibility exercises, which they believe contribute to external youth and long life. And it is clear that these exercises directly influenced the development of Chinese boxing. In Chinese medicine, it has long been believed that *chi* ("vital force" or "life force") resides in the body, and that *Tao*, the generative power of the universe, permeates everything. From these philosophical assumptions, the Chinese devised methods of breathing out the old or used spirit, and breathing in the new. The oldest breathing methods are based on four combinations of long and short inhales and exhales, and all are performed through the lower abdomen.

A famous doctor, Hua T'o, who lived in Wei at the time of the Three Kingdoms (220–280 A.D.), made a detailed study of the animal world, and sought to learn the secrets of the strengths of the various animals he observed. Since all of us, human and beast alike, receive our vital force (*chi*) from the great generative force (*Tao*) of the universe, Hua T'o reasoned, it should be possible for humans to "tap in" to some of the unique force received by the animals. Accordingly, he devised a series of exercises based on the movements and breathing patterns of various animals. These exercises he called "five animals at play," and they were based on the movements of the tiger, bear, monkey, deer, and eagle. These exercises, in turn, purportedly became the foundation of Shao Lin Temple boxing.

As Chinese boxing developed over the centuries, it became known as *chuan-fa*, and it developed along two distinct lines of thought and action. Of the many different systems of *chuan-fa* that existed at the time of their introduction to the Ryukyu Islands, each could be clearly classified as either *nei-cha* (internal systems) or *wai-cha* (external systems). Internal systems were characterized by soft, usually slow movements, and were devoted to the development of *nei-kung*, or "internal power." This internal power was developed through meditation and special exercises, which purported to stimulate the glandular and nervous systems. The manifestation of this internal power in combat was produced by a combination of will power, vital energy (*chi*), and muscular strength. The external systems, by contrast, were more vigorous in their practice and application, and they relied on *wai-kung* (external power) for their effectiveness in combat. These influences can be seen in the development of Okinawan boxing in *Shuri-te*, an external system, *Naha-te*, essentially an internal system, and *Tomari-te*, a combination of the two.

While Shotokan karate-do today has its metaphysical and philosophical aspects, it clearly derives from *wai-cha*, external systems, and relies most heavily on *wai-kung*, or external power. And as Okinawan boxing began to develop on its own, it moved farther and farther away from the Chinese "internal" concepts. Indeed, a good contrast can be drawn between the development of Chinese tai chi and Okinawan boxing. Tai chi during the Sung Dynasty (960–1279 A.D.) is typical of a Chinese system that originated as a healthful exercise form, developed into a martial art, and then returned to its original exercise form. Okinawan boxing, on the other hand, was developed surreptitiously for the purpose of survival. The Okinawans

faced an immediate need for survival, and the development of external power for the purpose of killing was their sole motive. While the courtly Chinese practiced their philosophical rites to commune with nature, the plebeian Okinawans banged their fists on boards and stones to make their hands strong enough to kill their oppressors.

In their physical appearance today, Chinese and Okinawan arts are easily distinguishable. The clearest contrast between the two lies in the performance of their formal exercises (in Japanese, *kata*). While the formal exercises of Chinese boxing are performed slowly, over 20 or 30 minutes, or sometimes even an hour or more, the Okinawan (and now Japanese) *kata* are performed in 45 to 75 seconds.

It is partly because of this quickness and vitality of karate that Westerners are more likely to be attracted to it than they are to the Chinese systems. In the West, we want to learn quickly, see immediate and measurable results, and then show our friends how good we are. But even though karate may appear easier and/or more rewarding on the outside, it is still incumbent on the practitioner to delve into the depths of karate as a martial way that can lead to a positive and fulfilling life. We must not be lulled into believing that because we can perform quick, fancy tricks, we are therefore masters qualified to teach others.

Indeed, the essence of karate as an artistic endeavor lies, according to Gichin Funakoshi, in the inner recesses of the human spirit, and it is to the search for this essence that we must apply our energies.

3

"Wakarimashita." "I understand, but..."

As this is being written, only a few Americans have been practicing karate-do under Japanese masters for almost 30 years, and some of them still say, "I just don't understand *Sensei*. Sometimes he's warm and friendly, and sometimes he's so distant, I can't reach him. Why doesn't he just say what he's thinking?"

The Japanese response to this is that Americans are too brash in their attempts to Americanize karate-do, and that 30 years is not nearly enough time to digest and assimilate the tenets of a culture that has developed in a straight line over several thousand years.

Both sides in the dispute have well-reasoned points of view, but neither is acknowledging the fundamental problem: Americans are not Japanese, and Japanese are not Americans, and fundamental changes in the art are not going to occur overnight.

It does seem clear, however, that if Americans will apply themselves assiduously to the task of better understanding the Japanese point of view, a new, truly Western aesthetic of karate-do and other martial arts might be born very quickly—perhaps within less than 100 years. One hundred years is a very short time in which to digest and change a facet of a culture which has developed steadily over more than 2,000 years.

Nevertheless, a study of the traditional Japanese view of life and Japanese society in general will lend itself to a better understanding of karate-do as it is now practiced, and further

39

study will help build the important bridge between Eastern and Western thinking.

One of the most readily apparent differences between East and West, and the difference that causes the most difficulties for Americans, is the Japanese concept of *tate shakai*, or "vertical society." *Tate shakai* means that the entire Japanese society is based on a system called *oyabun-kobun*. *Oya* means "parent," and *ko* means "child." Everyone in Japan understands this system, and most adhere to it. It is a system that not only defines the parent-child relationship, but also defines the boss-employee relationship and the master-follower (or master-retainer) relationship.

Oyabun-kobun is endemic to Japanese culture, and within this overall system is the specific system of *sempai-kohai* (senior-junior), which is prevalent in the *dojo*. *Sempai-kohai* is the structure of seniors and juniors, which is based upon education, economics, and time. In every relationship, every Japanese knows who is *oyabun*, who is *kobun*, who is *sempai*, and who is *kohai*. In the *dojo*, *sempai-kohai* most often is based on who has been training the longest, or rather, who has the most experience. Regardless of physical skills, the person with the most experience is always regarded as *sempai*, and the person with lesser experience is regarded as *kohai*. The *sempai* has responsibilities for the development of the *kohai*, and the *kohai* has responsibilities for tending to the needs of the senior members. The *kohai* always carries the *sempai's* bags, for example, and the *sempai* will never try to escape from the responsibility of offering advice and criticism to the *kohai*.

The whole system of *oyabun-kobun* and *sempai-kohai* is regulated by *mibun*—the Japanese system of rights and responsibilities. No one can have absolute authority over another without a concomitant share of distinct responsibilities. What is most often missed by Westerners in this system is that *mibun* carries with it an implicit restriction on the ingenuity and actions of the juniors. That is, an American who comes up with a unique and innovative idea has been conditioned from birth to selfishly copyright and patent that idea, and to take advantage of the Horatio Alger system of success. Within the system of *oyabun-kobun* and *sempai-kohai*, however, the junior is expected to selflessly present ingenious ideas to the senior, and the senior is expected to be sure that the junior gets credit. A junior who creates an innovative training method, for example, humbly presents that method to his senior, and if the senior likes the idea and uses it, he will be forthright in telling others that his junior invented it. In this way, the junior gets credit for his idea, and the senior gets credit for having such a good and faithful junior. If, on the other hand, a student invents something new and starts using it, looking for admiration and personal praise, he will be considered "a nail sticking up," and the senior will be obligated to hammer him back down into his proper place.

This is obviously in conflict with American thinking, but it is an honest and natural outgrowth of the Japanese concept of

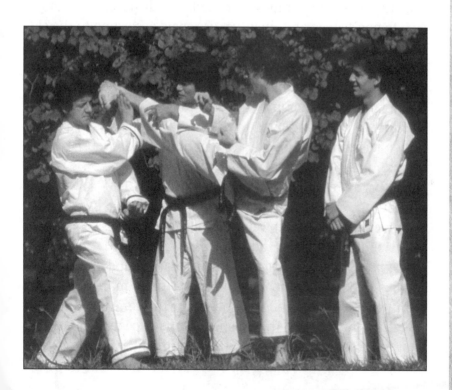

on, or "universal obligations." *On* is the word used in Japan to describe the universal obligations the Japanese have to one another, and which are passively incurred. According to Japanese thinking, one "wears an *on*" or "receives an *on*." *On* received from the Emperor is *ko on*, and *on* received from one's parents is *oya on*. *On* received from one's teacher is *shi no on*. When one receives *on*, the person who bestows it becomes one's *on jin* or *on* man.

Within the concept of *on* is the concept of *giri*, which is each individual's personal code of duty, honor, and obligation. As noted earlier, each level of society has its own *giri*, and it is believed that this *giri* is the most important facet of life.

Giri may be thought of as debts incurred toward one's *on jin*. In the sense of obligations to one's Emperor (*chu*), obligations to one's family of parents, ancestors, and descendants (*ko*), and obligations to one's work (*nimmu*), *giri* is considered *gimu*, which means that the duty of repayment is endless and that no matter how much is repaid, it will never be enough. *Giri* to one's associates, however, is repaid according to the significance of the *on* received, and it must be repaid promptly.

Another, distinctly different, kind of *giri* is the *giri* that each Japanese feels toward his name. This includes the duty to never admit failure or ignorance, the duty to live within one's means, the duty to clear one's name when it has been sullied, and the duty to refrain from displays of emotion in inappropriate situations.

If this system of *on* and *giri* were simply that—a system of obligations, duty, and honor—the Japanese would be very easy to understand. *Giri*, however, is made less accessible to the Western mind by the paradox of *ninjo*.

Ninjo is the concept of human feelings, and the concept implies that those human feelings are vastly more important than what is logical and profitable. For the time and effort he invests in the student, the Japanese *sensei* expects that the student will understand *tsukiai*, the social debt incurred by the student toward the *sensei*. In times past, *tsukiai* might mani-

fest itself in the students taking care of the *sensei's* every need. They would provide clothing, food, shelter, and whatever else he and his family needed.

Even this cursory overview of a few, selected, deeply held Japanese beliefs should serve to convince any Westerner that there is indeed a yawning gap between the thinking of East and West. But we have not even yet considered the most fundamental element of the Japanese psyche, the concept of *amae*.

Amae is, according to the majority of qualified Western and Eastern observers alike, the fundamental element of the Japanese psyche. It is the foundation upon which is built the entire history and evolution of Japanese thought and culture.

Amae is, for lack of better definition, "indulgent love." In a very real sense, *amae* is infantile dependence. It is the characteristic of love that an infant receives from its mother. According to Takeo Doi, one of Japan's leading psychiatrists and author of *The Anatomy of Dependence*, the Japanese do not feel comfortable in any personal relationship that does not have the quality of *amae*. To the Japanese, *amae* means that complete confidence and trust are inherent principles of any personal relationship, and it means that they can act in an "infantile"

43

manner in the relationship. That is, just as a child can act in many different ways, both good and bad, and still be assured that its mother will indulge such behavior, so do the Japanese expect a similar indulgence from one another. Just as a child can be rascally and raucous, and still be assured of the love of its mother, so can Japanese adults presume upon the indulgence of one another with impunity.

According to Doi, whose book was published in Japanese as *Amae no Kozo* (*The Structure of Amae*), the Japanese have a fragile inner core in their personalities, surrounded by many thick layers of emotional shells. Americans, on the other hand, have a very thick, strong inner core, surrounded by a very fragile, emotional shell. The slightest emotional disturbance or even a minor infraction of a social rule might shake an American visibly and thoroughly. The same actions, to a Japanese,

might elicit no response at all. In this sense, the Japanese are better "insulated," psychologically, than their American counterparts.

Several important qualities of *amae* are grossly misunderstood or misinterpreted by many Americans—even by those who have been training in karate-do for three decades. The first of these is *shinyo*, or "trust." In the sense of trust and confidence, *shinyo* means that in the *amae* relationship, a Japanese will perform his duty and fulfill his *giri*, regardless of the circumstances, cost, or personal inconvenience. *Shinyo* coupled with *enryo* (the holding back of feelings and emotions, "seeing things from a distance") sometimes causes the Japanese to seem cold, distant and aloof, when in fact he is probably just fulfilling a portion of his *amae* relationship with another.

This is not to say that the Japanese are not sometimes purposefully distant, cool, aloof, or outright hostile. Indeed, when an *amae* relationship is denigrated, or when one party unjustly takes advantage of another, the Japanese will express *uramu*—hostility that is justified by the actions of the party who has not observed the rules of *amae*.

Uramu often turns into *giseisha*, the "victim mentality," and when one party has grossly violated the *amae* relationship, *giseisha* is often used as a justifiable reason for revenge. What is important to understand in this regard is that this revenge (in feudal times, perhaps a vendetta) is not considered unjustifiably hostile or aggressive. It is, in fact, necessary for the preservation of the social, psychological, and moral order. Revenge is regarded as a method for teaching an offender a lesson.

When Japanese businessmen are dealing with each other, they deal within the framework of *honne to tatemai*, the "framework of one's thoughts," and they prefer *yakusoku* ("verbal agreements") to written contracts. They live by *chokkan to ronri*, the virtue and superiority of intuition over logic. When faced with a difficult decision, Japanese businessmen will say, *"Jan-Ken-Pon,"* which refers to a paper-scissors-stone game

played with the hands and fingers to settle questions. To the Japanese, good logic is that which is cyclical and paradoxical—not linear or Aristotelian. Truth, they believe, is *koto to shidai ni wa*—truth that is relative to the particular circumstances and obligations of *amae*. Logic and truth, as the Japanese perceive them, are not based on concrete rules. They are based on natural laws and *kongen*, the essence of the universe. Truth and logic are discerned, they believe, by achieving *mushin*—the "no mind" of the Zen tradition. *Mushin* is the clear, unaffected state of mind in which, it is said, things can be perceived exactly as they are, without illusion or emotion.

Another vexing attitude of many Japanese born before 1945 is *jibun ga nai*, which means, literally, "I have no self." What this implies is that what is good for the group is far more important and relevant than what is good for the individual.

Jibun ga nai is not much in vogue in modern Japan, but it is a serious force to be reckoned with in many Japanese born before 1945. Coupled with the modern concept of *risshin shusse*, or "rise to eminence through success," it is a very powerful force indeed. *Risshin shusse* today is most often coupled with *ki ga sumanai*, which means, "My spirit is not satisfied." Together, these concepts present the Westerner with an individual who is committed to rise to eminence through success in his chosen field, one who will place the good of his company or art over and above even his own welfare, and one who, apparently, will never be totally satisfied with the limits of his success.

Ki ga sumanai, in particular, often appears to Americans to be a Japanese obsession with rank, size, and the compulsion to be number one in everything.

In a very real, practical sense, this assessment is accurate.

To Americans, and indeed to the rest of the world, the Japanese appear to be an extremely complex people who come from an extremely complex, multi-faceted society. Realistically, it is much easier for them to understand us than the other way around. If we take Takeo Doi's thesis as fact, we, with our thin emotional shells, are much easier to penetrate than they are.

Among the Japanese karate masters who have lived in the West for two decades or more, some have become more Westernized, and some have avoided such a condition at all costs.

What is likely is that neither the Japanese or Americans will bend much in the direction of adapting themselves completely to their adopted cultures.

What is necessary for the survival and transmission of true karate-do is that they both study each other carefully and with an open mind.

In time, East and West will move closer together, and the bridge between the two will be much shorter and stronger.

4

Modern *Budo*: Defeating the Ego

I n its modern manifestations, karate-do may be approached and examined, with or without its sport aspect, as physical education, as an incomparable method of self-defense, and as a spiritual discipline. While the needs and interests of each individual will determine the emphasis, the art really cannot be separated into completely independent elements. The three defined elements—physical education, self-defense, and spiritual discipline—are, like the *yin-yang* symbol, a unified whole, and the seeds of each are found in the others.

The major problem inherent in defining, describing, and delineating the tenets and benefits of karate-do is that the art by its nature defies delineation and quantification. Perhaps the best we can do is consider the possible positive results of intensive and serious study, and seek ways in which these positive factors might be enhanced by specific training methods and specific patterns of thought.

When we speak of karate-do as a "spiritual discipline," we are not using "spiritual" in the religious sense; rather, we mean it to be understood as the incorporeal essence of human beings which is composed of feelings, moods, and attitudes. As a spiritual discipline, karate-do is concerned with the interplay of these feelings, moods, and attitudes both within the individual and as they influence the conduct of the individual in society.

But the spirit of karate-do professes no dogma and requires no monastic vows. It is, more than anything else, a way for individuals to learn about their true nature and to move

through life in a positive, rather than negative, fashion. Only the individuals themselves can make karate-do a religious experience, and only if they want to.

In the Western world, it is better to keep karate-do in the realm of the personal, removed from religiosity and sanctimonious doctrine. Karate-do will function more efficiently for the Western world if it is used as a tool with which one can examine and repair personality traits, psychological anomalies, and personal relationships. Consequently, a person far advanced in the study of karate-do might better be described as "spiritful" than "spiritual."

At various points throughout his writings, Gichin Funakoshi described the various benefits and positive character traits obtainable through the study and practice of karate-do. Serious study of the art would, he said, lead the practitioner to a clear mind and conscience, devotion to justice, unselfishness, obedience and gentleness, strength of character, moderation, courage and fortitude, introspection, a humble mind and gentle manner, courtesy, integrity, and self-control. It is difficult to argue with the apparent benefit and inherent "goodness" of these traits, but it is difficult for most Westerners to accept at face value Funakoshi's extreme high-mindedness regarding an art in which the medium is the breaking of bones and the tearing asunder of sinews and flesh.

The Japanese make the distinction between the physical techniques of punching, striking, kicking, and blocking and the intrinsic, artistic character of the art by saying "karate-jutsu" for the former, and "karate-do" for the latter. *Jutsu* implies "technique," while *do* implies "way" or "path." Further, *do* is the Japanese transliteration of the Chinese *tao*, and the implications of following the *tao* are not lost on the Japanese.

Indeed, the primary purpose of training in modern *budo* disciplines should be to transcend the quest for mere perfection of technique in the physical sense, and to attain self-realization and self-perfection. Training should be, in the Zen sense, a total commitment to the master and the master's way of teaching. It

should be rigorous enough and consistent enough to allow the student to achieve the state of *mushin*—the "no mind" sought after by devotees of Zen. It is in this state that the body and mind will respond naturally and efficiently to any situation or event, without forethought or premeditated design.

The premier Western historian of Japanese martial arts, the late Donn Draeger, wrote that these ultimate goals are much more difficult to attain in modern *budo* than they were in classical *budo*, or in classical *bujutsu*. According to Draeger, the intrinsic nature of classical *bujutsu* centered around combat, discipline, and morals. This, he asserts, was changed to discipline and morals during the time of peace in Japan when the warriors still occupied the upper social stratum. When *bujutsu* gave birth to *budo*, the intrinsic nature was again changed to reflect elements of morals, discipline, and form, and modern *budo* reflects only discipline and morals.

Draeger's analysis stands as a rather scathing criticism of modern *do* forms, and whether he was right or wrong in his assessment remains a matter of opinion. But there is no denying that the classical emphasis on *seishi o choetsu*, or "transcending thoughts about life and death," is less meaningful to modern warriors, who are not facing the prospect of death

51

every day, than it was to the classical exponents who had to place their skills on the line to survive.

Perhaps the most important difference between the classical and modern disciplines lies in actual combat. In classical disciplines, a confrontation was *buai shinken shobu*, or "a fight to the death between equals." In modern disciplines, combat is thought of in terms of self-defense, which carries with it the implication that a skilled practitioner is facing an unskilled one.

Nevertheless, it is important for sincere and serious karate-ka (practitioners of karate) to set the example, in both technique and demeanor, which will keep karate-do separate from karate-jutsu, and raise the art to its highest, most meaningful levels.

If the art is to survive and bear fruit for modern people, the attempts to commercialize it and promote it through sensational shows must be opposed at every turn.

When people speak of karate as a macho activity that enables people to beat each other up, serious karate-ka must clearly and forcefully, both through actions and words, demonstrate that karate-do is completely different in intent and process from karate-jutsu.

As an art, karate-do in the *dojo* should reflect upon and illuminate common actions and events in daily life. The traditional tenets and benefits espoused by Gichin Funakoshi must be examined, and ways to actively encourage the development of these benefits in *dojo* training must be sought.

When Gichin Funakoshi spoke of a clear mind and conscience, he was not referring merely to unclouded thinking and the ability to follow the course of linear logic. Indeed, he defined a clear mind and conscience as a mind purged of evil and selfish thoughts, and our Western heritage denies us the hidden meanings inherent in Funakoshi's words. In the Eastern tradition of Zen and Buddhism, evil and selfish thoughts are defined (according to Philip Kapleau) as "notions of good and evil, daydreams, 'I love this, I hate that,' angry or resentful thoughts, stubborn opinions, needless judgments, unnecessary evaluations and conclusions, pointless discriminations, covetous and jealous thought."[1]

Clearly, this definition encompasses far more than our taken for granted definition of evil and selfish as delineated in the Ten Commandments, and there can be no doubt that Funakoshi had the Eastern definition in mind when he set down his thoughts. He was, after all, a Confucian scholar who was thoroughly schooled in the Chinese classics.

If it seems that Kapleau's definition is saying that we should not make judgments or evaluations or draw conclusions, it should be noted that he is decrying *stubborn* opinions, *needless* judgments, *unnecessary* evaluations and conclusions, and *pointless* discriminations.

What Kapleau is talking about is ego.

Ego, in the *budo* sense and the Zen sense, is the consciousness of "I and you" or I, you, and they (or it)," and it is the ego, more than anything else, which must be defeated and suppressed in order to achieve the clear, everyday mind of *mushin*.

Karate students often hear their instructors say, "Don't think; just do!" What the instructor is saying, really, is, "Don't use your conscious mind; respond naturally from your subcon-

scious." In combat, the value of this idea is very easy to appreciate. A reaction to an attack will be less effective and slower if it is based on intellection and the realization of possible consequences. A reaction that is natural and instant, on the other hand, serves the warrior well.

D.T. Suzuki said it better than anyone else when he said, "The Zen approach is to enter right into the object itself and see it, as it were, from the inside."[2] When we can do this, we become part of the object, and it becomes part of us.

The purpose of defeating the ego, therefore, is to eradicate the distinction between "I' and "it" and to realize that "I" and "it" are merely conscious details that serve only to slow us down, make us think, and, therefore, (in the *budo* sense) to suffer defeat.

Defeat of the ego is accomplished when the conscious mind delves deeply into the unconscious, perceiving all things as one, and forever destroying the line between "I," "you," "it," "they," and the rest.

By giving themselves over completely to their teacher, karate students can forget all about concepts of "myself," "others," "what I can or cannot do," and proceed to find the essence of their art. If they train diligently, throwing away all preconceived ideas of accomplishment, ranking, the winning of tournaments, the admiration of their peers, and all their opinions, they will have a chance to learn karate-do from the inside out, as a part of the art, and the art will be a part of them.

But to accomplish this requires several things. First, it requires that students divorce themselves of all their opinions and ideas, turn themselves over completely to the *sensei*, and just practice karate because it is there. No other reason for training will suffice.

Second, it requires that the *sensei* be utterly devoted to transmitting karate-do to his students in the proper way. The *sensei* must take the stance of the Zen master of long ago who said, "I have nothing to reveal to you by wise words. If I did so, you might later have cause to hold my words up to ridicule. My job is to give you 30 raps on the head whether you do it right or wrong."

Once these conditions are met, the student will have a chance to learn karate-do in its purest form, and will, if training becomes a serious lifetime endeavor, be able to reap all the rewards Gichin Funakoshi purported in his writings.

Obviously, the attainment of the deeper, more meaningful rewards of karate-do is not an easy or overnight task. Indeed, a lifetime of hard work is required.

Ways are suggested here in which the serious student of karate-do might begin seeking the deeper meanings of the art. The ways are not technical ways; rather, they are guidelines that may serve to develop the proper state of mind for training. Since they are not always obvious, it is natural that the search for them begin in places where these ways might be hiding, obscured by our conscious minds.

The search for these ways must begin in the spaces between the techniques.

5

The Spaces Between
the Techniques

The basic method of artistic endeavor of any *do* is to formalize common actions and events, elevating them to their highest levels of elegance, grace, symmetry, and unadorned beauty, and then to appreciate the beautiful nature of these actions and events. In the tea ceremony, for example, one formalizes the simple and common actions of bowing, eating, and drinking a simple cup of tea. A simple vase of flowers (or a single stem) is given great attention and is appreciated as a fine work of art. Something as simple as a *kanji* (calligraphic character) or a tea scoop is studied intently, not with the mind, but with the aesthetic sense of feeling, and a great elevation of spirit and appreciation is realized. In all Japanese *do* forms, "feeling" is far more important and valuable than technique. "Don't think; just do!" say the Zen masters and karate *sensei*. Break through the limits of your intellect and feel.

Elevating common actions, events, and objects to the level of artistic beauty requires that one develop and maintain the spontaneous mind, for the more we think, the more our mind "stops" on one point or another. And as the mind stops, we cannot maintain the natural feeling of ebb and flow with nature. Nature, after all, never stops. Like truth, it is always dynamic, on the move, changing, perpetuating. When the mind stops, it "gets out of synch" with this dynamic flow, and confusion and doubts enter the mind, obfuscating the true nature of what is before the eyes and senses.

If we wonder what could possibly be considered "common" about swinging a sword or punching and kicking, we must remember that such actions were indeed common, everyday actions for the samurai, and our art, karate-do, is derived from the samurai tradition. What was once used for killing is now used for the perfection of character.

For the samurai, the highest expression of his "true self" and, consequently, his art, was in the blade of his sword. The blade was treated with a reverence incomparable in Western history and tradition. For the modern karate-ka, the highest expression of "true self" and art is found in the *kata*. The *kata* is the blade of the modern karate warrior, and in the *kata* the karate-ka expresses his level of understanding and development, either positive or negative, both to himself and to observers. At an advanced level, feeling is again more important than technique. The outward appearance of the technique is of little importance; what is important is the state of the spirit of the karate-ka.

The concept of art in karate-do goes beyond the Western idea that art imitates life. Indeed, in true karate-do, as in the days of the great samurai, the art expresses life itself. In the *kata* can be seen the spiritual state, the heart, the mind, the body, and the soul of the karate-ka. While a great painter or sculptor or writer may be able to hide personal excesses and rages in his art, the karate-ka who seriously pursues his art from a high point of view will not be able to conceal even the least bit of rage or hatred or excess. These will all be revealed in the first few movements of his *kata*.

Just as truth itself is dynamic and can offer no fixed answers, the *kata* of each karate-ka is dynamic and cannot be expressed or performed in any one, fixed way. What is expressed as strength in one person will be expressed as weakness in another. The goal of the *kata* is to overcome the gaps in thoughts between the self and the action. The concept of "myself and others" is what Philip Kapleau calls the "fundamental neurosis."[1] To perceive oneself as separate and distinct, in form and essence, from the rest of humanity is, according to Eastern thought, a fundamental error in perception. If all of nature and all of the universe are one, cosmic whole, unified and without schism, how can one individual be said to be special and outside the universal whole?

This is the type of question that must be asked to help us begin our journey on the course leading to enlightenment. It is a question without a fixed answer. Indeed, logic and reason cannot answer it to the satisfaction of everyone. There are either many answers, or there are none.

If we can once and for all rid ourselves of the useless notion that "there must be answers," then, and only then, can we approach karate-do from a high point of view. Both Zen and Taoism reject intellectualizing and linear logic in favor of a "flashbulb" awareness of truth. While logic and reason and written explanations can describe the process of integration of physical and mental disciplines, they cannot make us "go through the process." And "going through the process" is what

karate and Zen and Taoism are all about. A traditional Chinese proverb says:

> To hear is to forget.
> To see is to remember
> To do is to understand.

In karate-do, "to do" is to go through the process, and that requires sweat, sore muscles, some bruises, some strains, and more than a few blisters on the feet. Without going through this process, one cannot truly understand the nature of the art. Karate-do is a physical art that can bear metaphysical and healthful psychological fruit if we encourage and allow it to do so.

The Zen master and poet, Basho, said that the purpose of Zen is to "walk freely between earth and heaven":

> The Great Path (*Do*) has no gates.
> Thousands of roads enter it.
> When one passes through its gateless gate
> He walks freely between earth and heaven.[2]

For Basho, the process was meditation, poetry, and toil in his daily tasks. The main "gate" was the *koan*. A *koan* is a story or seemingly illogical problem assigned to Zen students. Through meditation and the development of a spontaneous mind through hard work on their day-to-day tasks, the students use the *koan* as a focus point to help them break through the barrier of logical and illusory thought and reach enlightenment. In karate-do, the process is the same (students work hard on their techniques without thinking or rationalizing), but the gate is different. In karate-do the gate is *kata*.

Disciplines as diverse as karate-do, flower arranging (*ikebana*), and poetry share several common traits. They all call for and encourage calmness and a quiet and composed demeanor; they require extreme concentration; and they all require that their techniques be performed intuitively without consciously thinking about the details of the technique or the consequences. That is, what is done is done from a calm and steady spirit. It flows naturally from inside the human being. What we see on the outside, whether it be a karate *kata* or a flower arrangement or a poem, is a reflection of what is inside the individual. If the individual's spirit is in turmoil, it will be reflected in a jerky *kata* or disordered flower arrangement or an incoherent poem. If the individual's spirit is calm and steady, and the mind does not waste time thinking about the details of how to perform the technique, the results will be quite different.

All Asian arts, and particularly karate-do, are very much concerned with states of awareness, or states of attention. There are three basic states of attention that are significant in the development of an individual's art. One of these is the "directed" state of attention, in which the individual's conscious attention is directed to the details of a particular thing. That is, the mind concentrates on one point at a time. The second state of attention is the "diverse" state of attention. In this state, individuals pay little or no mind to details. They do not concentrate on any one, specific point; rather, they let their mind wander, taking in all their surroundings without paying particular attention to any specific thing. The third state of attention is a combination of the first two. It is the "combined" state of attention. In this state, individuals let their mind move freely, taking in all that is around them, concentrating on whatever detail seems important, but without letting the mind stop. They may concentrate on a specific point, but their mind continues to be aware of the general environment.

It is this third state which most closely resembles the ideal illustrated in the *yin-yang* symbol.

It is the state of ideal awareness in which the mind flows freely, moves dynamically (as the *yin-yang* sphere spins dynamically), and maintains an even but dynamic balance and tension between all the opposing forces. The opposing forces, in this instance, may be aimless thoughts, fear of an opponent, or concentration on a single factor.

In free sparring, for example, the mind must not be allowed
to concentrate on any one detail. It must be open and free and
dynamically mobile (like the spinning *yin-yang*). That is, it
must see the entire opponent and know the entire environment. In self-defense, this is even more important, particularly
when there is more than one opponent. General, or diverse,
attention must be given to the entire environment. But the
individual must, at the same time, be able to direct attention to
any specific attack coming from any direction. In free sparring,
it is important to concentrate on seeing the entire opponent. If
you concentrate on the opponent's feet, you will be punched; if
you concentrate wholly on the opponent's hands, you undoubtedly will be kicked. The ideal state of mind in free sparring,
therefore, is the combined state of mind. In this state, the mind
moves freely from diverse attention to the environment to
directed attention to whatever attack may come from the opponent. In terms of the *yin-yang* symbol, diverse attention may
be thought of as the whole circle, and directed attention may
be thought of as points within the circle. The ideal is to maintain a steady and dynamic balance between the whole circle and

the points within it. As a representation of the mind, for example, if one half of the *yin-yang* circle realizes the point of itself in the other half of the circle, any movement of the other half of the circle will cause movement of the first half away from the causal movement. In this manner, balance is maintained, and the circle remains dynamic rather than static.

In the Zen tradition, the combined state of mind, dynamic and balanced, is called enlightenment. It is awareness of one reality, as opposed to directed concentration on one specific part of a larger reality.

In karate-do, this balanced state of mind is often referred to as *mizu no kokoro* ("a mind like water"), or *tsuki no kokoro* ("a mind like the moon"). That is, just as the *yin-yang* circle is a unified whole, which is clearly aware of specific points within itself, the mind of the karate-ka must be clear and reflective, like the surface of undisturbed water, and it should reflect equally on all that is around it, as the moon shines down equally and softly on all that is beneath it.

In advanced free sparring, the opponents do not really oppose each other. Rather, like the *yin-yang* circle, they try to become part of the one, large, cosmic reality. And this reality is not limited to the bodies, minds, and actions of the people who are sparring. Part of this reality, for example, is birth and death. Free sparring is something that occurs naturally in between, but is still part of the same dynamic cycle of birth and death. In the symbolism of the water and the moon, a point is reached at which the water is so clear and the moon so illuminating that the reality and reflection can no longer be separated. Indeed, it is no longer necessary to separate the two: they are both part of the same reality.

In the simple act of punching, we can perceive, if we are open to it, a clear representation and actualization of the dynamic balance symbolized in the *yin-yang* circle. As one hand goes forward, the other pulls backward. As students progress, they no longer think of their arms as separate, nor of the punch in terms of one hand going out and the other coming back. Both actions become one, and take their natural place in the dynamic sphere of existence and action. In free sparring, one strives for the ideal state in which an attack automatically triggers a counter-attack. When everything occurs simultaneously, there is no winner and no loser. In fact, two people so tuned to the movements of each other would probably not be able to move at all. They simply would stand motionless. This is what happened between the karate masters, Takayuki Mikami and Hirokazu Kanazawa, at one of the early All Japan Karate Championships. Through many overtime match periods, they stood motionless, each waiting for the other to show an opening in spirit or concentration. Ultimately, they displayed the ideal of the perfectly balanced dynamic sphere and became true representations of "motion in stillness." In the end, the tournament judges acknowledged their understanding of this unusual phenomenon by awarding both men the title of champion for that year. It was true karate-do: there were no winners and no losers.

The objective of the combined state of mind, then, is to perceive oneself and one's opponent as the same, and to see no difference between the two. Also, there is no difference between oneself, one's opponent, and the environment. They are all part of one, large, cosmic reality, and all will ebb and flow with the ebb and flow of the universe. This is what karate masters mean when they say, "Don't think; just do!"

For individuals to become one with their opponent and their environment, they must first become one with their own technique. In achieving oneness with their technique, karate masters will no longer display ego or fear (both illusory fabrications of a directed mind) or directed attention to specific factors in the environment. And while the process of achieving oneness with one's technique is supported by free sparring, it is largely derived from the practice of *kata*.

There is an ongoing controversy in the Western world over the necessity of practicing *kata*. People who are interested mainly in fighting, often say that practicing *kata* is a waste of time. Opponents of this position usually say that *kata* is the essence of karate-do, and the practice of physical techniques is best done in a formalized, structured manner. Neither of these viewpoints is completely correct, and both miss the main value of *kata* training. The point they both miss is that the main value of *kata* training is not necessarily the development of physical techniques.

While *kata* were originally devised to remember and practice techniques in a logical fashion, their main value for the modern, advanced karate-ka lies in the spaces between the techniques. As in our definition of the combined state of attention, successful performance and correct understanding of a *kata* requires that individuals let their mind move freely, taking in all that is around them, concentrating on whatever detail seems important, but without letting the mind stop. They may concentrate on a specific point, but their mind continues to be aware of the general environment.

It is true, of course, that we can learn a great deal about our physical bodies by practicing *kata*. We start our training with basic techniques and learn the basic ideas of momentum, driving motion, snap, rotation, and shifting, and we amplify these principles in our mind by practicing them in the *kata* in varied directions and with varied timing. But far more important than this is what the *kata* can teach us about our imagination, about timing (both internal and external), and about developing continuity between the actions of the mind and the actions of the body.

In a deeper sense, serious *kata* training can provide karate-ka with solutions to dilemmas—solutions that otherwise might elude them. For example, good karate-ka are expected to be bold and confident, and at the same time humble and gentle. In times of severe stress, they are expected to display a calm and steady demeanor. The attainment of these goals is very difficult to achieve in free sparring. When we spar with an opponent of greater skill, it is very easy to display humility and gentleness, but very difficult to express boldness and confidence. Similarly, when we face an opponent of lesser skill, it is very easy to be confident and bold, but there is little in the opponent's actions that will lead us to humility and gentleness. In such circumstances, we feel like we are one half of the dynamic *yin-yang* sphere: we can see our own point in the other half, but the other half will not cooperate in our attempts to change it.

In *kata*, on the other hand, we always control the opponent. We create him, we make him do what we want him to do, and we can make him do things that we would not want an actual opponent to do to us. In performing the *kata*, we can, with our imagination, make the opponent bold or shy, strong or weak, fast or slow, and we can learn to deal with many different types of opponents. In the spaces between the techniques, we have the opportunity to develop continuity between our techniques and to perform the techniques in varied circumstances with varied direction and timing. The *kata* gives us an ideal set of

circumstances in which to practice flowing from one technique to another. When we face an actual opponent, there is no time to stop and think and feel what should be happening in our bodies and minds. In the *kata*, however, we can do all these things, because we are sparring with our own imagination. Whatever our imagination conjures, we face. And we can face a

devastating opponent again and again, suffering defeat without damaging physical effect. And if we keep facing that opponent over and over again, we may eventually defeat him. The sense of accomplishment and overcoming of fear derived from this type of training is stored in the individual's intuition and memory, and can be called forth in an actual combat situation.

We can take this very seriously if we remember that fear of an opponent does not lie in the opponent or his actions, but only in the mind of the one who is afraid. Fear resides in the same realm with imagination, and, with discipline, we can make it come and go as necessary. Therefore, we should be deadly serious in *kata* training, and use the very best parts of our imaginative powers to create and deal with vicious opponents.

If we train conscientiously in this manner, free sparring becomes an extension of *kata*. What we face in our imagination, we retain in our intuition and memory, and we bring this forth to deal with an actual opponent when we spar. If *kata* training is done seriously, consistently, and with great imagination, all we will have to learn from sparring is distancing and timing. And even these factors will be far less complex when they are learned from a position of physical strength, which is a natural by-product of serious *kata* practice.

On both the physical and mental planes, the study of *kata* is the quintessential element of true karate-do.

6

Kara and *Ku*:
Emptying the Mind

More than 200 years ago, the Zen master, Kosen, wrote the calligraphy for "The First Principle" on a large scroll. This scroll was used by carpenters to trace the characters on a large piece of wood, which was then etched and draped over the gate of the Obaku temple in Kyoto. This plaque still hangs over the temple gate today, and is often referred to by modern calligraphers as "the great masterpiece."

When Kosen was working on the original calligraphy, one of his senior students, an audacious lad who thought more of himself than others, happened to pass by. Examining Kosen's work, he boldly proclaimed it "terrible" and "unfit as a pattern for a plaque."

Somewhat irritated by the criticism, Kosen tried again.

"Awful," said the student. "The first one was better."

In a controlled rage, Kosen proceeded to produce character after character, until more than 80 large sheets of paper lay scattered about, none of which was good enough to receive the approval of the student.

Driven to the brink of distraction by the young man's impertinence, Kosen's calligraphy began to look amateurish.

"I can't take it any more," sighed the student. "I'm going out for a drink of water, and then I'll be back."

"Now's my chance," thought Kosen. "I'll do this calligraphy without that young smart-aleck's approval!" Turning to the paper, Kosen dipped his brush in the ink, and with a mind com-

pletely free from the distraction of his pupil, quickly wrote, "The First Principle."

Just then the student returned. Looking at the calligraphy, he bowed deeply to Kosen, saying, "That is a great masterpiece!"

This famous story of Kosen and "The First Principle" has probably been told by more Zen masters to their pupils than any other over the past 200 years. This is not surprising, since it is a simple and perfect illustration of *mushin*—the clear, empty, unaffected state of mind sought after by devotees of Zen. In a state of *mushin*, it is said, one can respond naturally to any situation or action, intuitively feeling the true sense of the situation or act, without consciously thinking about it.

For the samurai warriors, the idea of responding naturally, calmly, and efficiently from a mind unencumbered by distractions or thoughts of fear, was obviously a very attractive idea. It enabled them to face their enemies boldly and, they believed, to

move in accord with the flow of the universe. In short, it made them almost invincible.

When Gichin Funakoshi was about to pass on, he left his pupils with 20 precepts which, he told them, contained all the "secrets" of karate. What his followers have learned is that the 20 precepts are timeless, sometimes confusing, and always challenging. Funakoshi, of course, is the man who lived his life by the motto, "The ultimate aim of the art of karate lies not in victory or defeat, but in the perfection of the character of its participants."

Clearly, Funakoshi intended for his followers to seek deeper meanings in their art, and not to be satisfied with mere physical skill. His precept, *Kokoro wa hanatan koto wo yosu*, or, "Always be ready to release your mind," is a good illustration of one of the "secrets" of karate-do which is not always evident in modern tournaments and exhibitions. It is, like the story of Kosen, an illustration of "The First Principle."

Prior to 1936, the Japanese characters representing karate were written with a character for *kara* that could also be pronounced "T'ang" or "*to*," and referred to the T'ang dynasty of China. *Te* means "hands." Thus, karate was the art of "Chinese hands." But Funakoshi decided that the Okinawans had been too anxious to call the art Chinese, and that now it was clearly Japanese in nature. In addition, Funakoshi steadfastly maintained that karate was a *do*, a path to follow for a correct, rewarding, and fulfilling life.

In an effort to correct the misinterpretation of karate as a Chinese art and at the same time to more clearly indicate the nature of the art as a way of life, Funakoshi changed the character for *kara* from T'ang to *ku*. *Ku* is also pronounced *kara*, and is found in the *Hannya Shingyo*, a Buddhist sutra containing the phrase, *Shiki soku ze ku, ku soku ze shiki*. In this phrase is contained the essence of karate-do, the way of life of the empty hand. Literally, it means "Form becomes emptiness, emptiness becomes form."

Shiki is the visible, physical form of a thing. It is the outward appearance of anything, such as a technique or a *kata*.

Ku is a term similar to the *mu* of *mushin*, and it means "emptiness." But *mu* is a specific term relating to the thinking processes of the mind, while *ku* refers more generally to the state of being, without any regard to form. *Ku* acknowledges existence, but describes an absence of form in that existence.

Ku is difficult to describe, but easy to feel. For example, as we go about our daily business, concentrating on our work or studies or whatever, there is a larger process occurring all around us, which we never examine, but which we notice and accept. That larger process is the change of seasons. As spring turns to summer, the weather becomes warmer, and one day we

notice that it is uncomfortably hot outside. As summer turns to fall and then winter, we become aware of the changes in temperature, and suddenly we realize that it is cold. If we go to bed on a clear night, we may be surprised to awaken in the morning and learn that a heavy snow has fallen. This change from season to season is *ku*; the seasons and the changes clearly exist, but they do not rely on conscious action. We do not contribute to the changes of season with our consciousness, nor are the seasons themselves "aware" of their own changes. The process of change from one season to another has no *shiki*, no visible form, but this process still clearly exists.

In karate-do, the meaning of *kara* (*ku*) is the same. For example, when students first learn a *kata*, they must concentrate on the movements, immersing themselves completely in conscious attention to every detail. A great deal of conscious thought is required, and complete attention must be given to *shiki*, the physical form of the *kata*. After many repetitions, however, the students do not consciously think so much about the physical nature of the movements; the movements become more natural, and the body remembers the sequence. The form (*shiki*) is becoming emptiness (*ku*). *Shiki soku ze ku.*

After thousands of repetitions (Funakoshi believed that at least three years of solid practice was necessary to master a *kata*), the *kata* becomes part of the nature of the student. When we watch masters perform a *kata*, we sometimes feel that they are moving in another plane of existence. They are no longer doing the *kata*; the *kata* is "doing itself" on their body. No conscious thought is given to the physical form of the *kata*. This complete emptiness (*ku*) is the same emptiness involved in the change of seasons. No conscious thought is involved, and the *shiki* (the different seasons or the techniques of the *kata*) is expressed through this emptiness. *Ku soku ze shiki.*

In the *kata*, Kanku Dai, the first movements are visual representations of *shiki soku ze ku, ku soku ze shiki*. The hands move together and raise above the head to look at the sky, then break apart, moving in a wide arc to come together again in

front of the center of the body. Together they are form; apart they are emptiness. Then they come back together. Form becomes emptiness, emptiness becomes form.

In the Zen tradition, pupils are taught that *shiki soku ze ku, ku soku ze shiki* means that positive becomes negative, hot becomes cold, gain becomes loss, and so on. The phrase is an exposition on the belief that the universe is dynamically balanced and in a constant state of flow between its polarities.

In karate-do, the expression of form through emptiness can only be found in the process of repeated performance of the techniques. Modern fighters are often heard to say, "Practice this or that technique until it becomes 'your second nature.'" But in its ultimate manifestation, the technique that has been practiced thousands of times is not a "second nature" tech-

nique at all. It is, in fact, an outward representation (*shiki*) of the manifestation of the emptiness (*ku*) of the performer. *Ku soku ze shiki*.

The benefit of this state of mind in free sparring, or in a real fight, is that the mind does not have to think about the situation nor devise a strategy for one kind of opponent or another. Indeed, in time of crisis, students who have trained rigorously to achieve this state will simply "release their mind," throwing out all conscious thoughts, allowing the techniques they have practiced so often to be performed through their body. No matter what the opponent does, the response of the student will be proper and strong, and it will often appear that the response comes before the attack. We have all heard about masters who "seem to know what I'm going to do before I do it," and *shiki soku ze ku, ku soku ze shiki* is the reason.

We can no more successfully attack such a person than we can stop the snow from falling by punching at the sky.

It is impossible to attack emptiness

7

Wabi and *Sabi*

*"How much does a person lack himself, who feels the
need to have so many things."*

— Sen no Rikyu, Tea Master to Nobunaga Oda
and Hideyoshi Toyotomi

The Grand Inter-Galactic Karate Tournament championship match was about to begin, and the finalists were decked out in glorious splendor. On the one hand was a husky, powerfully built fellow whose hair hung just past his shoulders onto a red, white, and blue uniform top, which was speckled with stars. His belt was black and two inches wide, and was adorned with four hot pink stripes on one end and his apparent nickname, "THE KID," in bold letters on the other. His opponent, somewhat less husky, but also powerfully built, was dressed in a royal blue *gi* top and black pants. A more modest sort of fellow, he carried on his back the name of his karate school and his instructor in silver letters four inches high. The collars and cuffs of his uniform were striped in red and white, and his trousers bore at least six patches on one leg. Some of the patches apparently represented organizations to which the fighter belonged or of which he was particularly fond. Others (some of which were Asian calligraphy, and one of which read, "HI-TEST") had more obscure meanings. But the most interesting part of his uniform was the jacket sleeves. The promotional brochure for the tournament had billed this event as a traditional event, and admonished contestants to wear "only approved karate *gi* with jackets extending below the belt, and

sleeves past the elbow." His sleeves did indeed extend to the middle of his forearms, but they were slit open from cuff to shoulder to reveal massive biceps—a ploy no doubt designed to intimidate opponents.

* * * *

While the name of the tournament described is fictional, the characters are real, and they are representative of the trend in modern American karate to make everything more fancy, more colorful, more memorable. Not only is this trend seen in the sartorial splendor of designer uniforms, but also in the modern wave of "free-form *kata,*" in which contestants are judged largely on their acrobatic abilities and choreographic skills.

And how, one might ask, does this relate to Sen no Rikyu, the tea master? The answer is that it does not relate to him at all, and that is the problem.

What the Japanese call true karate-do arose from a culture whose every facet was in some measure a reflection of the philosophy of Zen. From architecture to flowers and food, Japan's culture is a Zen culture, and karate-do is a reflection of that culture.

It is clear to any casual observer that Americans and other Westerners practicing modern karate seem to enjoy dressing themselves in lavish, colorful costumes, while virtually all of the revered Japanese and Okinawan masters of the art appear in simple, plain, white cotton uniforms, usually adorned only with a faded or ragged belt. The Japanese have words to describe this simplicity, and the words spring from the Zen tradition. The words are *wabi* and *sabi,* and they have no literal equivalents in English.

Wabi is perhaps best described as "intentional understatement," and it is a word that can be used to describe the essence of the Zen influence on Japanese art, architecture, flower arranging, tea ceremony, and even karate-do. Zen is a concept that de-emphasizes rational, emotive thinking in favor of a flashbulb-like awareness of the nature of things. Through meditation and activities unencumbered by the ravages of rational and emotional conscious thoughts, Zen devotees seek to clear their mind completely, emptying it of illusions, and to pierce the barriers of subjectivity and objectivity.

At its best, according to Zen tradition, the world is confusing, and the more we consciously think about the confusion around us, the more confusing it becomes. Zen decries the search for meaning and reality in individual actions and concerns; it calls for a completely empty mind which can perceive that individual actions and concerns are merely small reflections of a larger, cosmic reality. When people attain the empty mind (*mushin*), it is said, they will be able to find their own meaning in everything. This concept is a bit easier to grasp by considering Zen art.

Art that springs form the Zen tradition is not explicit in that the artist rarely draws a complete, detailed picture of the subject. What is drawn or painted is usually incomplete or unbalanced, and serves as a suggestion of the subject. The suggestion is that there is something missing, that if we will just open our minds to it, we will find something more about the subject if we try. It is as if the artist is telling us that since the world itself is imperfect and confusing, art should be a reflection of that

imperfection and confusion. No ultimate perfection is available in the world, and Zen art reflects this. But this is not to say that the Zen artist is sloppy and inefficient. Indeed, great skill and rigorous discipline are required to make things look "perfectly unbalanced" and incomplete. It requires disciplined restraint to create paintings or pottery or flower arrangements that are simple and elegant, and it is this disciplined restraint that is the simple and elegant nature of *wabi*.

The white, unadorned karate *gi* is a perfect example of *wabi*. It tells us nothing about the skill or nature of the person wearing it. It gives us no indication of his or her ability, and it does not confuse us with elaborate designs, flowing lettering, or informative patches. Since it is white, it symbolizes purity—the purity of motives of the person wearing it. Such people do not set themselves apart from others with memorable costuming. Rather, they acknowledge with their white *gi* that they are fundamentally the same as everybody else, and that their performance will have to speak for itself. In this sense, we, the spectators, are left to fill in the gaps and, just as when we view a simple character drawn by a Zen master, we must see for ourselves if there is more to this person.

Occasionally, we are given a clue by the condition of the belt the person is wearing. If it is old and worn or tattered, it can be a beautiful example of *sabi*, the beauty inherent in the patina of age.

Within the concept of *wabi*, the feeling of disciplined restraint, there is always an effort to express the sense of *sabi*, the feeling that age and imperfection lend beauty and dignity to an object of art. Again, great skill is required on the part of the potter to produce a teacup or a bowl that is beautifully imperfect, but still perfectly functional. Edges that are not quite round and lines that are not quite straight give the art a sense of reality and more accurately reflect on the imperfection of the world and the person who created the object. If a teacup or bowl is made by a machine, it may be perfectly symmetrical and without flaw. It is that very symmetry and perfection that make

it clear that a machine made it. When people make teacups and bowls, on the other hand, the object will bear the distinctions of the imperfections of the maker.

Similarly, when true karate masters perform a *kata*, they do so as if they were in a different time continuum. They do not rely on their costume to express their nature through the *kata*. When the *kata* has become a part of them and they a part of it, they express the movements of the *kata* with the disciplined restraint of *wabi*, and the confidence of having been with this *kata* a long, long time. The *kata* performance takes on *sabi*, the radiant glow of age.

In *kumite* (sparring), the principle is the same. The simple white *gi* tells the opponent nothing at all about the individual wearing it. The unmarked belt gives no hint as to the individual's experience, except in that it has color and may be a bit faded and worn.

Originally, karate-do, a product of Zen culture, was meant to be this way: two individuals facing each other to test heart against heart, spirit against spirit, technique against technique. It was the ultimate test, in that neither opponent knew anything of the other, and there was no outward appearance to give a clue to the other's nature. In their plain and simple uniforms, the contestants could commune with each other as small parts of a larger cosmic whole.

Today, however, these idealistic concepts are not much in evidence in many karate tournaments. Indeed, a great deal of brain power is devoted to developing concepts that explain the necessity of wearing one type of *gi* or another. Some insist that patches on the *gi* serve as a target for the opponent; others say that patches serve to distract the opponent. One bright fellow recently explained in great detail how black *gi* pants enable the karate-ka to sneak kicks in on an opponent, because black does not reflect light as well as white, and the opponent will therefore not see the kick coming. And at least two large organizations market a *gi* top specifically designed to confuse the opponent with its geometric design.

One must wonder how all of these modern theories might be viewed by the peasants who took their stance against gloriously armored samurai on the roads of Okinawa several hundred years ago. Many of them died there, but many samurai also perished in the bloody, brutal birth of karate. Perhaps brightly colored outfits would have helped the peasants, but perhaps what is lacked in depth of understanding is reflected in modern innovations.

Perhaps Sen no Rikyu was right.

8

The Masters Speak

I consider myself to be a very lucky person. Over the past 45 years, I have had occasion to meet and observe many of the greatest masters of many different martial arts, and each has been fascinating in his own way.

Koichi Tohei, the famous aikido master and founder of Ki Society International, captured my imagination with his sparkling personality, and Takashi Kushida, Chief Instructor of Yoshinkai aikido in North America, dazzled me with the incredible precision and brilliance of his technique. Thirty-five years after meeting Shoshin Nagamine, the founder of Matsubayashi Shorin-ryu karate, I feel just as overwhelmed today as I did the day I met him. His demonstration of technique was overshadowed by the awesome aura of his personal presence.

I have seen demonstrations by Gogen Yamaguchi, founder of Japanese Goju-ryu karate, Hironori Ohtsuka, founder of Wado-ryu karate, and Kenei Mabuni, son of the founder of Shito-ryu karate.

In Shotokan karate, my chosen art, the list of masters I have met or observed closely is virtually endless: Nakayama, Miyata, Nishiyama, Okazaki, Asai, Kase, Kanazawa, Ozawa, Mikami, Yaguchi, Koyama, Tanaka, Takagi, Itoh, Shirai, Oishi, Enoeda and others.

While all of these people have very clearly defined individual personalities and specific ideas about their art, it is clear to me that they all share a common bond: all of them believe they are practicing *budo* because *budo* is the way of virtuous people.

I have written about many of these people over the years, and I have selected the thoughts of three truly outstanding

karate masters for inclusion here. Each of these men is extraordinary in his own way. Each has legions of followers and vociferous detractors. Masatoshi Nakayama was revered as the outstanding, traditional Japanese karate master and, until his death in 1987, the most senior active student of karate's founder, Gichin Funakoshi. Hiroshi Shirai and Takeshi Oishi are held in high regard as masters and competitors who reached the zenith of their competition careers at a time when karate was changing from its more traditional methods into a modern art for mass consumption. All of these men, I believe, are true karate masters, and though they all come from different generations and different backgrounds, I believe the most important ideals of karate-do are reflected in their words and their lives.

Some of them have engaged in academic research on the ideals of karate-do, and some have not. All of them in their own way, however, are living examples of the attainment and continuing pursuit of the ideals of karate-do.

An Interview with Hiroshi Shirai and Takeshi Oishi

We are honored to present this interview with two of the greatest karate men alive, Mr. Hiroshi Shirai and Mr. Takeshi Oishi. A profile of these two men, both instructors for the Japan Karate Association, reads like a "Who's Who" of competition karate.

Mr. Shirai began his karate training under Hidetaka Nishiyama in 1957, and received his basic training while majoring in Geography at Komazawa University in Tokyo. While his original goal was to become a high school teacher, he responded to Mr. Nishiyama's personal request to enter the JKA Instructor School in 1961. He immediately entered tournaments and gained a formidable reputation in competition. Entering his first All Japan Championship in 1961, he captured 2nd place in the individual *kumite* (free sparring) division, and followed in 1962 with 1st place wins in *kumite* and 2nd place in

kata. So impressive was Shirai's ability, he was chosen to represent the Tokyo district in the 1962 All Japan Selected Athletes Tournament, where he again overwhelmed his competition and placed 1st in *kumite* and 2nd in *kata*. He rounded out his competition career in 1963 with 2nd place wins in both *kumite* and *kata* at that year's All Japan Championship. In 1965, Shirai was chosen, along with famous champions Enoeda, Kanazawa, and Kase, to tour the U.S., Europe, and South Africa, demonstrating the highest levels of JKA karate-do to the world. In November of 1965, Mr. Shirai moved to Italy to become the Chief Instructor for the JKA in that country, and today holds the positions of Technical Director, Executive Director and Vice-President of the Federation Sportiva Italiana Karate. Mr. Shirai holds the rank of 7th *dan* from the JKA.

Takeshi Oishi, has literally become a legend in his own time. Originally trained in kendo in high school, Oishi entered the JKA Instructor School upon graduation from Komazawa University with a degree in Economics in 1965. Following his appointment as a lecturer in the physical education department at Komazawa, Oishi entered the 1967 All Japan Karate Championship and captured 2nd place in the *kumite* division. In 1968, he placed first in *kumite* in the World Invitational Championship in Mexico City and 1st in the International Goodwill Matches in Los Angeles. In 1969, 1970, and 1971, Oishi was by far the strongest fighter in Japan, taking 1st place in the All Japan Championships each year. He did not compete in 1972, but dashed all newcomers' hopes by winning again in 1973. He captured 1st place in *kumite* in the All Japan Selected Athletes Tournament in both 1970 and 1971. In the WUKO World Championship in 1972, Oishi was undefeated at the time of the withdrawal of the Japanese team from the competition, and placed second behind teammate Masahiko Tanaka at the IAKF World Championship at Los Angeles in 1975. Since 1977, Oishi has been the Chief Coach of the World Champion Japanese Karate team, and serves as Assistant Professor of Physical Education at Komazawa in Tokyo, where he resides with his wife and two children. Mr. Oishi holds the rank of 6th Dan from the JKA.

The interview with these two extraordinary men was conducted during the 1977 AAKF Special Summer Training Camp in San Diego. Special thanks are extended to Dr. Jacques Perrault for assistance in conducting the interview, to Mr. Torajiro Mori for coordinating the meetings, and to Mr. Ken Tambara for his excellent assistance with translation.

Question: *What are your impressions of the U.S. in general, and the karate you have observed here, as compared to the karate in other countries?*

Shirai: I have the general impression of great enthusiasm among the American karate people I have observed, and I think this is directly attributable to the personality of Mr. Nishiyama and the high standards he sets for himself and his students. As far as karate in other countries is concerned, I really can't speak with authority about Japan, because I have been away from there for over 12 years. In Europe, however, there was a great karate boom several years ago, and the public became widely exposed to the art. We have a great number of students left from the boom, but they have only a very limited knowledge of karate. They understand the basic techniques, but they lack in-depth training, and that is what we are working to correct now. We want each club director to be trained more in-depth about the more advanced physical and philosophical aspects of the art. In the United States, I think the training is more in-depth, due to Mr. Nishiyama's exacting and precise

instruction. Most of the instructors here rank in at least the 2nd or 3rd *dan* and have received very detailed instruction from Mr. Nishiyama. In Europe, because so many people are training, a student becomes an instructor almost as soon as he is promoted to 1st *dan*, and the instruction remains relatively shallow. As I say, this is the main subject we are concentrating our efforts on.

Mr. Oishi, what is your assessment of the levels of competition among the various countries today?

Oishi: I would like to say at the outset how pleased I am that European and American karate people have such good manners and respectful feelings for karate. In some cases, they show better manners than many of the Japanese. Technically, Europeans are exhibiting incredibly high quality in their techniques, and I think the Americans I have seen are superior even to them in the exactness and precise quality of their techniques. In Japan, at the JKA headquarters, preciseness of technique is, as it always has been, the main subject of study. The Japanese, therefore, remain significantly ahead of the rest of the world in the quality of techniques. They cannot help but be ahead. As far as competition goes, I think the strongest teams outside of Japan are the Italian and Argentine teams, with Italy having the edge. I don't say this because Mr. Shirai is here, but I have been in karate a long time, and have spent a good deal of time in Europe, and the Italians have now and will continue to have, I believe, the cleanest, strongest techniques in Europe.

More specifically, what about the competition levels?

Shirai: I hesitate to qualify karate athletes just in terms of competition, because that is not the point of karate. I do not compete in tournaments anymore, but I still do free sparring for the sake of doing it as a part of my karate development. And that is how I would prefer to categorize other karate students. Competition is not the main point, and I can say this because I have a long history of tournament competition and a record as a "champion." Practicing karate strictly for competition is not practicing karate at all—it is practicing to get the point in a tournament, and the two are not the same. Even though I have long experience in competition, I still do free sparring all the time with my students, but not with the intention of winning tournaments. I spar to broaden my experience. The most important point to remember is that if one does strong karate consistently—basics, sparring, and *kata*—the matter of competition will take care of itself. It is better to have strong techniques that cannot be blocked than to have a few tricks that are designed to score points. Realistically, there is so much to do and learn in karate that there simply is not enough time to train just for tournaments. One must build up his own body and build the muscles to perform the techniques. And hard work is necessary to build up a harmony between the physical and psychological self. And all of this requires the building up of a strong fighting spirit that makes you go forward even though you might die. Distance, timing, and experience facing other people are the key elements to success in competition, and these elements are comparatively simple to master when they are emphasized in general training. *Kata* practice is an exercise in developing the harmony between mind and body, which is essential in free sparring. Also, in *kata* one must always have the image of opponents in his mind and perform the *kata* as if he were actually being attacked. And while *kata* training has nothing to do directly with tournament fighting, it is important to carry over the feelings from the *kata* to the competition match and express the techniques against actual attack. I feel happiest not when my students score the highest points in a match, but rather when I see the student expressing his techniques in terms of his own personality, from the depths of his own human spirit.

Do you think there is a danger in placing emphasis on competition?

Shirai: That depends entirely on the attitudes advertised by the organizers of tournaments and the quality of the referees

93

and judges. If the judges are highly qualified, I don't think there is any inherent danger in having tournaments. And of course the contestants must be trained properly and in the proper spirit.

Oishi: I am not adding much to this, because I was trained by Mr. Nishiyama and Mr. Shirai, and I agree with them totally on this point. I would say that for myself, my competition training consists of exactly the general training Mr. Shirai describes, with the addition of perhaps 10 minutes of training in timing exercises after each class. And in the class, I always try to move faster than the other people when I hear the count. Not faster, really, but with a quicker starting motion. At the universities in Japan, the people are forced to "get the point" in a match in order to move up, and I see a great danger in that kind of training. The pressure for this kind of training sometimes prevents me from teaching what I feel is true karate, and I think it would be disastrous if the rest of the world began training like that.

Shirai: Yes, and that is why we must keep Mr. Nishiyama's idea of highly qualified organizers and judges in mind.

Oishi: The most important thing is for the person to understand the meaning of karate and to practice it consistently. No matter what condition a person is in, he must train as often as possible and do his best to do good *kata*. That is the essence of karate.

Could each of you tell us something about how karate fits in your personal lives and how it affects your lives outside the dojo?

Shirai: When I started karate, I did it because it fascinated me, but that really is not why I continue to train. I do karate to improve my personality. I believe that through training in the techniques and philosophy of karate, I can deepen the capabilities of my human self—physically, emotionally and spiritually. Right now all I do is karate. Even when I am old and cannot do what I do now, I will still continue teaching karate until I die. I feel an obligation to my *sensei*, Mr. Nishiyama, to inherit and carry on the good karate he teaches me, so that it will not die.

Oishi: I find great purpose and challenge in studying and understanding one thing completely. But it is not easy. When I go back to Japan, Master Nakayama and Master Shoji make me train very hard in the classes, and because I am 37 years old, I sometimes get discouraged and think, "Why should I do this? I am 37 years old and should be entitled to slow down a bit." But some time ago I had an injury and had to watch the classes rather than participate, and that almost killed me. I wanted to train so bad I almost could not stand it. I just can't stand watching; I love to participate. And there is one, main goal I want to accomplish: I want to reach the levels Mr. Nishiyama and Mr. Shirai have reached, and be as good as they are when I am that age.

One final question. What advice would you give to Americans who are now studying karate?

Shirai: I would say that whatever environment you are in, you will encounter difficult problems that do not appear to have solutions. But if you keep training in karate, you will have something to cling to—an inner strength that will carry you through the difficult times and help you find the solution.

Oishi: I agree. And I would add that so many times I wanted to quit karate during hard times, but staying with it got me through. It is very fulfilling and rewarding, and continuing always is the main point. And especially those who decide to become instructors should give themselves over to it completely. There is a Japanese phrase that applies here: "*Shu-ha-ri.*" "*Shu*" means to follow everything the master says; "*ha*" means to examine what the master has taught and decide that some things are not very good or simply could be improved; "*ri*" means to completely break away and establish your own system. This is the cycle of a man's life, for if the master's teaching was correct and if the man is honest, he always finds himself back at the "*shu*" stage, doing the basic things all over

again. I have been in karate for over twenty years, and I am still in the *"shu"* stage. It is very important to choose one *sensei* and do exactly as he says—stay with him to the end.

Shirai: It is very important to accept what the *sensei* says without reading anything into it or taking anything away from it. Accept what the *sensei* says directly, and follow it exactly.

Oishi: Yes, but even though I always do exactly what my *sensei* says, I really want to do better than him. I want to make a stronger punch and a stronger kick than Mr. Nishiyama and Mr. Shirai, and this is a strong motivation to follow what they say. I want to prove to them that I can do it better. I can't do it better, of course, but I still try. That is the point of training in karate under a good *sensei*.

One Step at a Time
The Story of Masatoshi Nakayama

This is an article of historic significance. It is based on extensive discussions between the author, himself a JKA instructor as well as an accomplished writer, and Masatoshi Nakayama, head of the Japan Karate Association, the largest martial arts style organization in the world. Nakayama is called "Master" by over 6 million karate students.

He is 69 years old. He has practiced karate for 50 years. He studied both in college and privately with Gichin Funakoshi, founder of Japanese karate; and—a nearly unknown fact—he studied kung fu for almost a decade in China. He is truly a pivotal figure in the worldwide development of martial arts.

Until now Nakayama has never been on the cover of any major American magazine, nor has he granted an in-depth interview before this to any American martial arts publication. —Ed.

A lot of lip service is given to "character development" these days in the martial arts. A cursory glance at the yellow pages in any major city informs the reader that, in addition to all physical benefits, karate training will give "self-confidence," "self-

control," and "perfection of character." While these clichés serve to add an aura of mystery and respectability to the karate schools, many new students rapidly (and painfully) become aware of the fact that the methods employed to develop all this character and self-confidence often revolve around a hub of "rock-'em, sock-'em, beat-'em-up, and see how many pushups they can do before they pass out." Those who survive and ultimately win their black belts take solace in the fact that someday they, too, will be able to develop "character" and "self-confidence" in new members.

Masatoshi Nakayama, ninth degree black belt and headmaster of the Japan Karate Association (JKA), also has a lot to say about character development and self-confidence, but his methods are definitely from another world. He says, "The true purpose of karate is not the winning of fights or tournaments. The true purpose of karate is to perceive the truth of life through daily training, and to gain self-confidence and self-reliance."

If this sounds like typical lip service, it should be noted that at the age of 22, Nakayama, acting on the charge of his teacher, Gichin Funakoshi, sought the truth of life by journeying on foot through Mongolia, across the Greater Khingan Mountains, into Outer Mongolia. With only his daily karate training to sustain him, he wandered through the steppes of Outer Mongolia, lonely, afraid and hungry. After four months of arduously seeking spiritual awakening and inner strength, Masatoshi Nakayama overcame his fears and obtained self-confidence and self-reliance.

Lip service indeed! This man does not spew out empty clichés; he speaks from direct experience in karate—experience that is virtually without peer.

Born to a family of fencing instructors in Yamaguchi City, Japan, in 1913, young Masatoshi Nakayama received most of his elementary education in Taipei, Taiwan. His father, Naotoshi, was an army surgeon and kendo master who introduced his son to kendo while Masatoshi was still a child. While in Taiwan, the young Nakayama was very athletic. In elementary school, he ran sprints on the track team, swam every day, and played tennis. Upon returning to Japan and entering middle school, he concentrated his energies on kendo and skiing.

"By the time I was ready to enter the university," he says, "I was fairly proficient in kendo. So, when I arrived at Takushoku University, I immediately checked the schedule to see when the kendo club practiced. But I misinterpreted the schedule, and when I got to the *dojo*, there were a bunch of men in white uniforms practicing strange, dance-like movements. One of the older ones came over and told me that they were practicing karate, and if I liked what I saw, I could try it at their next class session. I had read something about karate in the newspapers, but I didn't know much about it, so I decided to sit down and watch for a while. Very shortly, an old man came into the *dojo* and began instructing the students. He was extremely friendly and smiled at everyone, but there was no doubt that he was the chief instructor. On that day, I got my first glimpse of Master Funakoshi and karate. I decided that I really liked him and that I would try karate at the next class because, with all my kendo background, it would be easy. At the next class, two things happened that changed my life: First, I completely forgot about kendo, and second, I found that karate techniques were not at all easy to perform. From that day to this, I have never lost the sense of challenge inherent in trying to master the techniques of karate-do."

From those inauspicious beginnings 50 years ago, Masatoshi Nakayama has pursued his challenge with a vengeance. The author of more than 20 books on karate, Nakayama is today the chief instructor to more than 6 million JKA members around the world, having been personally chosen by Gichin Funakoshi to pass on JKA Shotokan karate-do to the rest of the world.

Gichin Funakoshi, the man who introduced karate to Japan from Okinawa, was a man of foresight and vision. When young Nakayama walked into his *dojo* in 1932, Funakoshi immediately

perceived that there was something special about this young man, and he moved quickly to develop Nakayama's potential.

"The training sessions under Master Funakoshi," Nakayama recalls today, "were very strict and rigid. During class sessions at the University, Funakoshi Sensei would watch us while we

Photo by Tom Openlander

performed technique after technique, hundreds of times each. Then he would select a *kata*, and we would repeat it 50 or 60 times. This was always followed by intense practice on the *makiwara* (padded striking post). Master Funakoshi himself would join us at the *makiwara*, and I can remember him striking the *makiwara* as many as 1,000 times with his elbows. During my first year in training, he invited me and several others to come to his house in the evenings, after our studying was finished. In his back yard, he had a small wooden deck built as an outdoor training area. Every night I would go to his house with two or three other students, and we would practice some more under the Master's supervision. Sometimes we would practice our *kata* until well after dark, and we had to be careful not to bump into each other."

This extraordinary apprenticeship continued without abatement until 1937, when Nakayama left Takushoku University and set out to fulfill a dream he had nurtured all his life: he went to China to study Chinese language, society and history.

"I went to Peking as an exchange student," he says, "to study Chinese language (Mandarin), society, and history. And wouldn't you know it?" he laughs, "One of the first things I saw in China was Chinese boxing! At first, I wasn't very impressed with the Chinese arts as fighting methods. They emphasized circular movements, and they had no *kime* (focus) like Japanese karate, so I thought they were weak."

But his early opinions changed rapidly.

"I once saw an instructor receive a broken arm from what appeared to be a soft, circular block, and I decided that I must look deeper into the Chinese martial arts."

And look deeper he did. For 10 years he studied many different styles of Chinese martial arts.

"As time went by," he says, "I learned that the Chinese arts had a lot of value. The history of China is long and deep, and so is the history of her martial arts. The Chinese martial arts have great depth."

As might be expected, Nakayama did not confine his study of the Chinese arts to an academic overview.

"I trained very hard with many different instructors, and since I was also teaching karate, an art they had never seen, many of the instructors got to know me fairly well. In fact, when a Japanese newspaper sent a film crew to do a story about Chinese martial arts, *sifu* (teachers) from all over China came to demonstrate for the cameras, and they asked me to act as their interpreter. As a courtesy to me, they also insisted that I demonstrate karate, so I did. In my demonstration, I emphasized *kime* and *kata*.

"At this time, Japan and China were on the verge of war, and it was rather disconcerting to see the Japanese and Chinese newspapers squabbling over which country had the best martial arts. The Japanese said that Chinese boxing looked pretty, but lacked speed and *kime* and was obviously no good for fighting. The Chinese retorted that while karate appeared to be fast and strong and extremely powerful, it was still just a brand-new martial art and lacked refinement and depth. Since I was teaching karate to a lot of sincere Chinese students and they were teaching me kung fu and tai chi, we found the whole affair amusing."

Nakayama's study of Chinese arts, however, led to far more than amusement.

"I trained for a long time," he recalls, "with an 80-year-old sifu—a famous Peking boxer who was absolutely extraordinary with his legs. He seemed to be able to wrap his leg around an attacking arm, and his defensive movements were marvelous. As a result of studying with him, I developed two new kicks that were incorporated into karate techniques by Master Funakoshi when I returned to Japan. One is a pushing kick or block using the sole of the foot or the lower portion of the leg, and the other is the reverse roundhouse kick."

After five years at the university in Peking and several more years working for the Chinese government, Nakayama returned to Japan in 1946 to find his country in ruins from the war. Many of his training partners had been lost in the war, and the few of those who survived had not found much time to practice karate. Even worse, the General Headquarters of Allied Powers (GHQ) had banned the practice of all martial arts.

"They thought karate was a part of judo," Nakayama recalls, "but I went to the head of the Education Bureau at the Ministry of Education, and he helped us convince the allied powers that karate was not part of judo at all. Using the premise that karate was actually a form of Chinese boxing—a sport—we received permission to practice. The GHQ thought karate was just a harmless pastime! So, while the other martial arts had to wait until the ban was lifted in 1948, we were able to practice and progress."

By the fall of 1947, Nakayama had gathered together the remnants of the karate seniors in Japan, and they were again practicing daily under the watchful eye of Gichin Funakoshi. In May of 1949, they officially organized themselves into the Japan Karate Association with Funakoshi as their chief instructor and Nakayama as chief technical advisor.

In 1948, the U.S. Air Force base at Tachikawa invited Nakayama and several judo and kendo instructors to give a demonstration of their arts. So successful was this performance that Nakayama was called upon by other air bases to give demonstrations at the rate of two or three per week for the next three years. These demonstrations set the stage for the intro-duction of karate to America.

"The history of American karate really revolves around the decision of the Strategic Air Command (SAC) to teach martial arts to their personnel," says Nakayama. "In 1951, SAC sent 23 physical training instructors to the Kodokan in Tokyo to study the various martial arts under the leading instructors in Japan. This program continued for 15 years, and it exposed a large number of Americans to correct principles of karate, judo, aikido, and other martial arts."

Even more significant than merely introducing Americans to karate, was the impact that teaching the Americans had on

the Japanese. Until 1951, the teaching method of karate had been fairly simple: students imitated their instructors and repeated the movements over and over until they were perfect. The Americans, however, would have none of that; the Americans wanted to know why. "Why should my legs be here and not there?" "Why should I twist my arm when I punch?"

"It immediately became apparent to me and to Master Funakoshi that if we were going to teach Americans, we would have to provide a theoretical basis for our art," says Nakayama. "So, under Master Funakoshi's guidance, I began an intense study of kinetics, physiology, anatomy, and hygienics. We believed that with a thorough grounding in the scientific basis of body mechanics, we would find it easier to teach foreigners."

With all the contributions to karate that Masatoshi Nakayama has made, many believe that his greatest contribution by far is his theoretical basis of instruction. His system, summarized in his 1965 textbook, *Karate-do Shinkyotei* (A New Method for Teaching Karate-do), is now in use in JKA schools all over the world, and it has been copied by instructors in other organizations virtually everywhere. A much-condensed version of his book is popular in English under the title of *Dynamic Karate*.

Others argue that Nakayama's most important contribution to karate is the karate tournament. While others in other styles of karate were practicing various forms of free sparring as early as 1935, it was Nakayama who was largely responsible for devising the original rules for karate competition, and it was he who staged the first All-Japan Karate Championship Tournament in Tokyo in 1957.

"Prior to 1953," he says, "there were no organized public tournaments in Japan, or anywhere else, for that matter. In effect, our tournament in 1957 was the first world karate championship."

Paradoxically, as a pivotal figure in the development of sport karate and as head of an organization that has led the way

Photo by Tom Openlander

in internationalizing karate through competition, Nakayama has mixed feelings about karate competition.

"Early in my training," he recalls, "I and a lot of other young students wanted some form of combat. We just weren't satisfied with *kata* all the time. Even though he was reluctant, Master Funakoshi gradually began "introducing us to *sanbon* (three-step) and *gohon* (five-step) sparring, and finally *ippon kumite* (one-step sparring). I don't think he liked doing this,

105

because he was very adamant on the point that karate was not a barbarous, combative art. Nevertheless, by 1935, various college clubs all over Japan were staging what they called '*kokangeiko*' (exchange of courtesies and practice). These exchanges were supposed to consist of *kata* practice and one-step sparring with prearranged attacks and defenses. In reality, they often degenerated into brawls. I saw broken noses and jaws, teeth knocked out and ears almost ripped off.

"I was torn between the belief that karate needed a combative aspect and the sure knowledge that someone was going to be killed if this sort of thing went unchecked. I also saw judo and kendo flourishing as sports in the pacifistic climate of postwar Japan, and I was concerned that if karate continued on its bloody course, the people would reject it.

"My solution was to study the rules of many different kinds of sports, and to experiment with various ideas of competition. Once, for example, I set up matches in which contestants wore heavy padding and fought full-contact. The padding was designed on the order of kendo armor, but it was of course much lighter. To my great dismay, we found that the armor itself, because of its bulkiness and restriction of movement, caused more injuries than it prevented. Finally, the committee members and I came up with what we thought would be a viable set of rules for sparring, and Master Funakoshi approved them. We were all very saddened when he died just a few months before the first All-Japan Championship. He was looking forward to it, and he knew it would be the springboard for internationalizing karate.

"My greatest concern at that time was to ensure that karate, if given a sporting aspect, would not lose its essence as an art. I therefore worked very hard on designing *kata* competition, and I based the rules on the rules of skating and gymnastics competitions. My one hope was to preserve the essence of karate-do as an art of self-defense and self-denial, and to prevent the excitement of sparring from transforming karate into a mere sport."

Today, Nakayama feels his efforts were successful, but not without some reservations.

"The full-contact karate in America and Europe," he says, "certainly has a place in the world of karate, but it is not karate-do. *Do* means 'way' or 'path,' and it means that the art is a vehicle for improving human character. What is most important to understand is that this seeking after better character is not a temporary or fleeting goal. It is a life-long process that must be pursued every day through training.

"Sport," he emphasizes, "develops the contestants in a straight line. That is, they train hard in the physical techniques until they become strong, and then they compete. As they compete, they become stronger and stronger, and some become champions. But after a certain number of years, the body begins to decline, and the contestant can no longer compete effectively. One progresses steadily toward a narrow ideal, which is reached at the peak of youth, and then age brings a straight decline.

"Karate-do, on the other hand, has no such narrow ideal as the winning of championships, and human progress in the art is like climbing a series of stairs or steep steps. As the mind and body grow together, the student moves continuously onward and upward, one step at a time. Even when the body declines, there is still another step ahead in the seeking of character perfection. Until the day you die, the process is endless, because no one is perfect, but we can all become a little better if we keep trying.

"Full-contact karate," he continues, "is like boxing in that it is all based on force—the strongest person wins. While there is nothing wrong with that, and certainly nothing wrong with making contact, it is very important, I believe, to develop the human spirit through controlled techniques. This is one of the pillars of karate-do competition. Executing a fast, powerful technique and stopping it with perfect control and precision requires total control of the mind. In sport, the emphasis is on the strong body; in karate-do, the emphasis is on the mind.

107

Everything begins and ends with the mind, and this gives the karateka qualities he can carry over into his daily life and use to his benefit. This control also enables the karateka to control his blows with whatever force is necessary. In a self-defense situation, the thoroughly trained karateka will always find the

Photo by Tom Openlander

right distance, and the correct amount of force will be delivered to the target."

In listening to Masatoshi Nakayama talk about karate-do, it becomes apparent that he regards his art as an art of virtuous people, an art with an extremely high standard of ethics.

"The soul of karate-do," he says, "lies in Master Funakoshi's admonition, '*karate ni sente nashi*,' which means that there is no first attack in karate. But this does not simply mean that the karateka will not make the initial move to start a fight. Master Funakoshi repeatedly told us that it is also a strict prohibition against carelessly using the techniques of karate. This spirit is embodied in the *kata*, each of which begins with a defensive movement."

Expounding on the "no first attack" principle, Nakayama is very adamant in his belief that "This also means that a karateka should never act in a manner that could create an atmosphere of trouble, and he should avoid places where trouble is likely to occur. If a student frequents a bar where fights occur on a regular basis and he is suddenly called upon to use his techniques in self-defense, then he does not understand the meaning of *karate ni sente nashi*. In effect, he started the fight, because he knew trouble was likely, and he could have avoided the conflict altogether by simply not going there."

"*Karate ni sente nashi*," he says, "is a wish for harmony among people. In the *kata*, Kanku Dai, this wish for harmony is symbolized in the first movement, which is unlike any other *kata* and which does not relate directly to defense and attack. The hands are raised together above the head, palms outward, and the karateka looks at the sky through the hole formed by his fingers and thumbs. This movement expresses identification with nature, tranquillity of mind and body, and the wish for harmony. The karateka who understands this will have a modest heart, a gentle attitude, and a wish for harmony."

To observe this little man (Nakayama is not quite five feet tall) practicing his karate is to observe the human embodiment of the ideals he holds so dear.

109

During his recent two-month tour of North America and the Caribbean under the sponsorship of Teruyuki Okazaki and the International Shotokan Karate Federation, Nakayama visited many *dojo* and taught classes at a pace that would kill lesser men. At the *dojo* of Yutaka Yaguchi in Denver, 69-year-old Nakayama took off his *gi* top to show the black belts which muscles they should use in various techniques. One student, a nurse in her early 30s, commented, "In my nursing experience, I've seen a lot of 70-year-old bodies, but that's the first one I've ever seen that looked like it was 35!"

Indeed, Masatoshi Nakayama in his street clothes appears to be in his 50s; in his *gi*, blasting young black belts around the room with kicks and punches, he appears ageless.

The highest stage of karate-do, he says, is the transcendence of body and mind—a state in which the mind and body move freely and smoothly, regardless of age or physical condition. Though he would be reluctant to admit it, Nakayama's followers believe that he has reached this state and is moving even farther beyond. "He's just not like a regular human being," one instructor says.

For proof, his followers point out that Nakayama, also a master ski instructor in his capacity as chairman of the Physical Education Department at Takushoku University, was completely crushed by an avalanche while skiing in the Japanese Alps in February of 1971. The doctors gave him up for dead, and his family came to his bedside. There was no possibility, said the doctors, that a man of his age could survive such a catastrophe. Rather than die, however, Nakayama woke up after a few days and announced that he was hungry. Well, okay, conceded the doctors, he might live, but he will never walk again. When he left the hospital four months later and resumed his training at the JKA headquarters *dojo*, the doctors, like his many students, became astonished believers. "There is something special about him," one doctor said. "I can only attribute his recovery to his amazingly high fitness level, or perhaps to a miracle."

But to hear Masatoshi Nakayama tell it, it is no miracle, and he is nothing special: "Karate-do is attained one step at a time, and so is life. Just train every day and try your best, and the truth will come to you."

Appendix

The Timeless Ideals

A very clever instructor once told me, in a moment of great distress for me, "If I tell you, you won't know!" That statement was the beginning of my personal awakening to the deeper meanings of karate-do. I had already studied for a long time, and I had read widely, but in that instant it became clear to me that all the intellection I could muster would never be enough to truly internalize the meaning of the art I was pursuing.

Looking back over this volume, I am torn between the belief that the concepts discussed here need explaining, and the clear knowledge that explanation is merely an intellectual exercise that will never lead anyone to what may be called "the elevation of the human self." Only dedicated training in karate-do will do that.

So I leave the reader with the concepts that stirred my youthful interest so many years ago. These are the true karate ideals. They ask questions, they confuse, they stimulate, and they explain. They are the signposts along the pathway of karate-do, and they are the guidelines we strive to understand.

I. *Dojo Kun*

DOJO KUN
(Principles of the *Dojo*)

Hitotsu! Jinkaku kansei ni tsutomuru koto!
(One! To strive for the perfection of character!)

Hitotsu! Makoto no michi o mamoru koto!

(One! To defend the paths of truth!)

Hitotsu! Doryoku no seishin o yashinau koto!
(One! To foster the spirit of effort!)

Hitotsu! Reigi o omonzuru koto!
(One! To honor the principles of etiquette!)

Hitotsu! Kekki no yu o imashimuru koto!
(One! To guard against impetuous courage!)

II. *Myo wa kyo-jutsu no kan ni ari.*
(The perfect state of existence [*Myo*] lies between what is substantial and what is insubtantial.) or,
(The essence [of martial ways] lies in the balance between offense and defense.) or,
(The ideal state lies between guarded and unguarded.) or,
(The truly exquisite state of being lies between what is substantial and what is insubstantial.)

III. *Shu ha ri.*
(Obedience, Divergence, Transcendence.)
(The process of karate-do training is cyclical. One begins by blindly and faithfully obeying the master, then going one's separate way, and ultimately transcending the teaching and discovering something new. What lies beyond transcendence is obedience, and the cycle starts again.)

IV. *Ikken hissatsu.*
(One-punch death-blow.)
(The purpose of karate-do training is to develop each technique into a "one-punch death-blow." Each movement balances between life and death. There is never a second chance.)

V. *Do mu kyoku.*
(No limitation for life.)

(The path [*do*] of the student is endless, and there are no limitations.)

VI. *Mizu no kokoro.*
(A mind like water.)
(The karate-do student should develop a mind like the water on the surface of a clear, undisturbed pond. As the clear, calm surface reflects everything around it perfectly, so should the mind.)

VII. *Tsuki no kokoro.*
(A mind like the moon.)
(The karate-do student should develop a mind like the moon, which shines evenly on all before it, without harsh shadows and areas of glare.)

VIII. *Heijo-shin.*
(Everyday mind.)
(The karate-do student should develop a mind which is "normal" at all times—calm, centered and contemplative, regardless of the circumstances.)

IX. *Ju yoku go o sei suru.*
(Flexibility conquers hardness.)

X. *Kobo-itchi.*
(Offense and defense are one.)

XI. *Shingi ittai.*
(Mind and technique are one.)

XII. *Gichin Funakoshi's Twenty Precepts.*

SHOTO NIJU KUN
(Shoto's Twenty Precepts)

1. *Karate-do wa rei ni hajimari, rei ni owaru koto wo wasuruna.*
   (Karate-do begins with courtesy and ends with courtesy.)

2. *Karate ni sente nashi.*
   (There is no first attack in karate.)

3. *Karate wa gi no tasuke.*
   (Karate is a great assistance to [auxilliary of] justice.)

4. *Mazu jiko wo shire, shikoshite tao wo shire.*
   (Know yourself first, and then others.)

5. *Gijutsu yori shinjutsu.*
   (Spirit first; techniques second.)

6. *Kokoro wa hanatan koto wo yosu.*
   (Always be ready to release your mind.)

7. *Wazawai wa getai ni shozu.*
   (Misfortune [accidents] always comes out of idleness [negligence].)

8. *Dojo nomino karate to omou na.*
   (Do not think that karate training is only in the *dojo*.)

9. *Karate no shugyo wa issho de aru.*
   (It will take your entire life to learn karate; there is no limit.)

10. *Arai-yuru mono wo karate-ka seyo, soko ni myo-mi ari.*
    (Put your everyday living into karate and you will find the ideal state of existence [myo])

11. *Karate wa yu no goto shi taezu natsudo wo ataezareba moto no mizu ni kaeru.*
    (Karate is like hot water. If you do not give it heat constantly, it will again become cold water.)

12. *Katsu kangae wa motsu na makenu kangae wa hitsuyo.*
    (Do not think that you have to win. Rather, think that
    you do not have to lose.)

13. *Tekki ni yotte tenka seyo.*
    (Victory depends on your ability to distinguish vulnerable
    points from invulnerable ones.)

14. *Tattakai wa kyo-jutsu no soju ikan ni ari.*
    (The battle is according to how you maneuver guarded
    and unguarded. Move according to your opponent.)

15. *Hito no te ashi wo ken to omoe.*
    (Think of the hands and feet as swords.)

16. *Danshi mon wo izureba hyakuman no tekki ari.*
    (When you leave home, think that you have numerous
    opponents waiting for you. It is your behavior that invites
    trouble from them.)

17. *Kamae wa shoshinsha ni ato wa shizentai.*
    (Beginners must master low stance and posture; natural
    body position for advanced.)

18. *Kata wa tadashiku jissen wa betsu mono.*
    (Practicing a *kata* is one thing, and engaging in a real
    fight is another.

19. *Chikara no kyojaku, karada no shinshuku, waza no
    kankyu wo wasaruna.*
    (Do not forget strength and weakness of power, stretch-
    ing and contraction of the body, and slowness and speed
    of techniques. Apply these correctly.)

20. *Tsune ni shinen kufu seyo.*
    (Always think and devise ways to live the precepts every
    day.)

Notes

Notes for Chapter 1

Page 4–1. Hassell, Randall G. "An Interview with Hidetaka Nishiyama." *Samurai*, Autumn, 1978.

Page 5–2. Funakoshi, Gichin. *Karate-do Kyohan*. Tokyo: Kodansha International, Ltd., 1973.

Notes for Chapter 4

Page 53–1. Kapleau, Philip. *Zen: Dawn in the West*. Garden City, NY: Anchor Books, 1980.

Page 54–2. Suzuki, Daisetz T. *Zen and Japanese Culture*. Princeton, NJ: Princeton University Press, 1970.

Notes for Chapter 5

Page 59–1. op. cit.

Page 60–2. op. cit.

Glossary

A

akindo (chonin)	merchants
amae	"indulgent love"

B

bakufu	central government
buai shinken shobu	"a fight to the death"
budo	martial ways. The word *budo* is derived from characters meaning "the way to stop conflict."
budoka	one who practices *budo*
bugei	martial arts or arts of the warrior
buke	military class in Japan
bushi	professional warriors of feudal Japan
bushido	the way of the warrior. A formal code formulated in the 17th century.
bushi no ichi-gon	"the word of a *bushi* is inviolate"
bushi no nasake	"the tenderness of a warrior"

C

chi	Chinese word meaning "vital force"
chokkan to ronri	"intuition is more than logic"
chonin (akindo)	merchants
chuan fa	Chinese term meaning "fist way"

D

daimyo	provincial governors
dan	grade. In karate, used to signify black belt ranking
do	"way" or "path"
dojo	The place of the way. The place where the way of life is taught and studied.

E

enryo	the holding back of feelings and emotions

119

eta (hinin)	outcasts

G

gi	uniform worn in karate practice
giri	one's personal code of duty, honor and obligation
giseisha	the victim mentality

H

heimin	commoners
hinin (eta)	outcasts
hitotsuki hitogeri	"one punch, one kick"
honne to tatemai	the "framework of one's thoughts"
hyakusho	farmers

I

igen	dignity of demeanor
ikebana	flower arranging
iken hisatsu	"to kill with one blow"

J

Jan-Ken-Pon	a paper-scissors-stone game played with the fingers to settle questions
jibun ga nai	"I have no self."
jutsu	art or technique

K

kanji	calligraphic characters
karate-do	the way of life of the empty hand
karate-jutsu	the techniques (art) of the empty hand
karate-ka	practitioner of karate
kata	formal exercises
katana	long sword
kendo	the way of the sword
kenjutsu	the techniques (art) of the sword
ki ga sumanai	"My spirit is not satisfied."

kime	focus of physical, mental and spiritual energy
kizoku	peers
koan	a problem assigned to students by Zen teachers, which must be solved through direct perception rather than through logic or intellection
kobudo	the way of weaponry
kobun	the junior person in a relationship
kohai	the junior members of an organization or society
kokangeiko	exchange of courtesies and practice
kongen	"the essence of the universe"
ko on	obligations to one's Emperor
koto to shidai ni wa	"truth is relevant to circumstances and obligations"
ku	emptiness or void
kuge	court nobles
kyu	"class." In karate-do rankings, kyu is used to designate those below the black belt ranking.
kyuba no michi	the way of the bow and horse
kyudo	the way of the bow (archery)
kyu-jutsu	the techniques (art) of the bow (archery)

M

makiwara	"straw-wrapped rope" used as a pad for forging strong hands and feet through punching and kicking
mibun	the Japanese system of rights and responsibilities
mizu no kokoro	"a mind like water"
mudansha	"without grade" or "no grade" Used in martial arts to indicate those below the black belt level.
mushin	"no mind"

N

nei-cha	Chinese term meaning "internal system"
nei-kung	Chinese term meaning "internal power"

121

ninjo	human feelings

O

Okinawa-te	"Okinawan hands;" refers generally to empty-handed systems of self-defense developed on Okinawa
on	universal obligations
on jin	the person to whom one has an obligation
oyabun	the more senior person in a relationship
oya on	obligations to one's parents

R

risshin shusse	rise to eminence through success
ronin	"wave man;" masterless samurai
ryu	school or style

S

sabi	in Japanese aesthetics, the patina of age; rusticity
samurai	common name for professional *bushi*; derived from a word meaning "to be at one's side."
satori	enlightenment
seishi o choetsu	"transcending thoughts about life and death"
seishin no mono	"a thing of the spirit"
sempai	the senior people in an organization or society
sensei	teacher; literally "one who has gone before"
shiai	a *budo* contest; *shi* means "test" and *ai* means "come together." Thus, a *budo shiai* is a contest in which people "get together to test each other."
shiki	the visible, physical form of a thing
shin budo	modern (new) martial ways
shi no on	obligations to one's teacher
shinyo	trust
shizoku	in feudal Japan, the privileged class of gentry
shokunin	artisans
shu-ha-ri	a martial arts term literally meaning "Obedience, Divergence, Transcendence"

T

tachi	blade or sword
tanren	active, lifetime training to master the self
Tao	Chinese term meaning the way of the universe
tate shakai	vertical society
te	hand
tode	old name for karate. *To* is an alternate rendering of *kara*, and refers to things of Chinese origin.
tsukiai	the social debt incurred toward one's *sensei*
tsuki no kokoro	a mind like the moon

U

uramu	hostility

W

wabi	in Japanese aesthetics, the quality of simplicity, or intentional under-statement
wai-cha	Chinese term meaning "external system"
wai-kung	Chinese term meaning "external power"

Y

yakusoku	verbal agreements
yari	spear
yin-yang	Chinese term meaning "negative-positive"
yudansha	"with grade;" in martial arts, this is used to signify those who have attained the black belt ranking.
yumi and ya	bow and arrow

Z

Zen	transliteration of the Chinese ch'an; the process of concentration and absorption in which the mind achieves tranquillity and one-pointedness

Bibliography

Primary Written Sources

Adams, Andrew. Ninja: *The Invisible Assassins*. Burbank: Ohara Publications Incorporated, 1973.

Aitken, Robert. *Taking the Path of Zen*. San Francisco: North Point Press, 1982.

Arnold, Edwin. *The Light of Asia, The Life and Teaching of Gautama*. New York: Doubleday & Company, Inc., Dolphin Books Edition, 1961.

Barthes, Roland. *Empire of Signs*. New York: Hill and Wang, 1982.

Benedict, Ruth. *The Chrysanthemum and the Sword: Patterns of Japanese Culture*. New York: American Library, 1974.

Bergamini, David. *Japan's Imperial Conspiracy*. New York: William Morrow and Company, 1971.

Blyth, R. H. *Zen and Zen Classics (7 Volumes)*. Tokyo: Hokuseido, 1960–1966.

Burtt, E. A. (Ed.). *The Teachings of the Compassionate Buddha*. New York: The New American Library of World Literature, Inc., 1955.

Capra, Fritjof. *The Tao of Physics*. New York: Bantam Books, 1975.

Christopher, Robert C. *The Japanese Mind: The Goliath Explained*. New York: Linden Press/Simon and Schuster, 1983.

Conze, Edward. *Buddhism: Its Essence and Development*. New York: Harper Torchbooks, 1959.

Corcoran, John, and Farkas, Emil. *Martial Arts: Traditions, History, People*. New York: Gallery Books, 1983.

de Bary, William Theodore (Ed.). *Sources of Japanese Tradition*. New York: Columbia University Press, 1964.

_____. *Sources of Chinese Tradition*. 1964.

DeMente, Boye. *The Japanese Way of Doing Business*. Englewood Cliffs, NJ: Prentice-Hall, Inc. 1981. The Whole Japan Book. Phoenix, AZ: Phoenix Books, 1983.

Deshimaru, Taisen. *The Zen Way to the Martial Arts*. New York: E. P. Dutton, Inc., 1982.

Doi, Takeo. *The Anatomy of Dependence*. Tokyo: Kodansha International, Ltd., 1973.

Draeger, Donn F. *Classical Bujutsu*. New York: John Weatherhill, Inc., 1973.

_____. *Classical Budo*. 1973.

_____. *Modern Bujutsu and Budo*. 1974.

_____ and Smith, Robert W. *Asian Fighting Arts*. Tokyo: Kodansha International, Ltd., 1969.

Egami, Shigeru. *The Way of Karate, Beyond Technique*. Tokyo: Kodansha International, Ltd., 1976.

Enoeda, K., and Mack, C.J. *Shotokan Karate Free Fighting Techniques*. London: Paul H. Crompton Ltd., 1974.

Feng, Gia-Fu, and English, Jane (Translators). *Tao Te Ching*. New York: Random House Vintage Books, 1972.

_____. *Chuang Tsu*. 1974.

Fromm, Erich. *Zen Buddhism and Psychoanalysis*. New York: Harper & Row, Publishers, Inc., 1970.

Funakoshi, Gichin. *Karate-do Kyohan*. Tokyo: Kodansha International, Ltd., 1973.

_____. *Karate-do, My Way of Life*. 1975.

_____. *Ryukyu Kempo Tode*. Bukyo-sha. 1922.

Gard, Richard A. (Ed.). *Buddhism*. New York: Washington Square Press, 1963.

Hall, John Whitney. *Japan, From Pre-history to Modern Times*. New York: Delacourte, 1970.

Harrison, E. J. *The Fighting Spirit of Japan*. Woodstock, NY: The Overlook Press, 1982.

Hasegawa, Seikan. *The Cave of Poisonous Grass: Essays on the Hannya Sutra*. Arlington, VA: Great Ocean Publishers, 1975.

Hassell, Randall G. *Conversations With the Master: Masatoshi Nakayama*. St. Louis: Focus Publications, 1982.

_____. *Shotokan Karate: Its History and Evolution*. 1984.

Hearn, Lafcadio. *Japan: An Interpretation*. Rutland, VT: Charles E. Tuttle, 1955.

Herrigel, Eugen. *Zen in the Art of Archery*. New York: Random House (Vintage Books Edition), 1971.

Hirai, Tomio. *Zen and the Mind*. Tokyo: Japan Publications, Inc., 1978.

Hoover, Thomas. *Zen Culture*. New York: Random House, 1977.

_____. *The Zen Experience*. New York: New American Library (Plume Edition), 1980.

Humphreys, Christmas. *Zen Buddhism*. New York: Macmillan, 1949.

Ihara, Saikaku. *Tales of Samurai Honor*. Tokyo: Monumenta Nipponica, 1981.

Kanazawa, Hirokazu, and Adamou, Nick. *Kanazawa's Karate*. London: Dragon Books, 1981.

———. *Shotokan Karate International Kata* (2 Vols.). Tokyo: Shoto-kan Karate International, 1981.

Kapleau, Philip. *The Three Pillars of Zen: Teaching, Practice, and Enlightenment*. Tokyo: John Weatherhill, Inc., 1966.

———. *Zen: Dawn in the West*. Garden City, NY: Anchor Books, 1980.

Kennet, Jiyu. *Selling Water by the River, A Manual of Zen Training*. New York: Random House, Inc., 1972.

Legge, James (Translator). *The I Ching, The Book of Changes*. New York: Dover Publications, Inc., 1964.

Leggett, Trevor. *A First Zen Reader*. Tokyo: Charles E. Tuttle, 1960.

———. *Zen and the Ways*. 1987.

Mabire, Jean, & Breheret, Yves. *The Samurai*. London: Wyndham Publications Ltd, 1976.

Mattson, George E. *Uechiryu Karate Do*. Plymouth, New Hampshire: 1974.

Mishima, Yukio. *The Way of the Samurai: Yukio Mishima on Hagakure in Modern Life*. New York: Basic Books, 1977.

Morris, Ivan. *The Nobility of Failure*. New York: Holt, Rhinehart and Winston, 1975.

Morris, P.M.V. *The Illustrated Guide to Karate*. New York: Van Nostrand Reinhold Company, 1979.

Murakami, Hyoe, and Seidensticker, Edward G. (Eds.). *Guides to Japanese Culture*. Tokyo: Japan Culture Institute, 1977.

——— and Harper, Thomas J. *Great Historical Figures of Japan*. 1978.

Murakami, Hyoe, and Hirschmeier, Johannes. *Politics and Economics in Contemporary Japan*. Tokyo: Japan Culture Institute, 1979.

Miyamoto, Musashi. *The Book of Five Rings*. New York: Bantam Books, Inc., 1982.

Nagamine, Shoshin. *The Essence of Okinawan Karate*. Tokyo: Charles E. Tuttle, 1976.

Nakayama, Masatoshi. *Dynamic Karate*. Tokyo: Kodansha International, Ltd., 1966.

Nicol, C. W. *Moving Zen: Karate As a Way to Gentleness*. New York: William Morrow and Company, 1975.

Nishimura, Eshin. *Unsui: A Diary of Zen Monastic Life*. Honolulu: University Press of Hawaii, 1973.

Nishiyama, Hidetaka, and Brown, Richard C. *Karate: The Art of Empty-hand Fighting*. Tokyo: Charles E. Tuttle, 1960.

Nitobe, Inazo. *Bushido, the Soul of Japan*. Tokyo: Charles E. Tuttle, 1969.

Okakura, Kakuzo. *The Book of Tea*. New York: Dover Publications, 1964.

Okazaki, Teruyuki, and Stricevic, Milorad. *The Textbook of Modern Karate*. Tokyo: Kodansha International Ltd., 1983.

Perrin, Noel. *Giving Up the Gun*. Boulder, Colorado: Shambhala Publications, 1979.

Random, Michel. *The Martial Arts*. London: Octopus Books, Limited, 1978.

Ratti, Oscar, and Westbrook, Adele. *Secrets of the Samurai: A Survey of the Martial Arts of Feudal Japan*. Tokyo: Charles E. Tuttle, 1973.

Reischauer, Edwin O., and Fairbank, John K. *East Asia, The Great Tradition*. Boston: Houghton Mifflin Company, 1960.

Reps, Paul. *Zen Flesh, Zen Bones*. Tokyo: Charles E. Tuttle, 1957.

Rielly, Robin L. *Karate Training, The Samurai Legacy and Modern Practice*. Tokyo: Charles E. Tuttle Company, Inc. 1985.

Ross, Nancy Wilson. *Three Ways of Asian Wisdom*. New York: Simon and Schuster, 1966.

Sansom, George B. *A History of Japan* (3 Volumes). Stanford, CA: Stanford University Press, 1958-1963.

_____. *Japan: A Short Cultural History (Revised Edition)*. New York: Appleton-Century-Crofts, 1962.

Senzaki, Nyogen, and McCandless, Ruth Strout (Eds.). *The Iron Flute*. Tokyo: Charles E. Tuttle, 1961.

Shimano, Eido (Ed.). *Like a Dream, Like a Fantasy: The Zen Writings and Translations of Nyogen Senzaki*. Tokyo: Japan Publications, Inc., 1978.

Storry, Richard. *The Way of the Samurai*. New York: Mayflower Books, 1978.

Stryk, Lucien, and Ikemoto, Takashi (translators and editors). *Zen: Poems, Prayers, Sermons, Anecdotes, Interviews*. Garden City, NY: Doubleday and Co., Inc., 1963

Suzuki, Daisetz T. *Zen and Japanese Culture*. Princeton, NJ: Princeton University Press, 1970.

_____. *Manual of Zen Buddhism*. New York: Grove Press (Evergreen Edition), 1960.

_____. *Zen Buddhism: Selected Writings of D. T. Suzuki*. New York: Doubleday, 1956.

Suzuki, Shunryu. *Zen Mind, Beginner's Mind*. New York: John Weatherhill, 1970.

Suzuki, Tatsuo. *Karate-Do*. London: Pelham Books Limited, 1967.

Tsunetomo, Yamamoto (Translated by William Scott Wilson). *Hagakure, The Book of the Samurai*. Tokyo: Kodansha International, Ltd., 1979.

Turnbull, Stephen R. *The Samurai: A Military History*. New York: Macmillan Publishing Co., 1977.

van de Wetering, Janwillem. *The Empty Mirror*. New York: Pocket Books, 1978.

_____. *A Glimpse of Nothingness*. Boston: Houghton Mifflin Company, 1975.

Waley, Arthur. *Three Ways of Thought in Ancient China*. New York: Doubleday Anchor Books, (no date). First Published 1939.

_____. *The Way and its Power, A Study of the Tao Te Ching and its Place in Chinese Thought*. New York: Grove Press (Evergreen Edition), 1958.

_____. *The Analects of Confucius*. 1939.

Williams, Bryn. *Know Karate-Do*. London: William Luscombe Publisher Ltd., 1975.

_____, ed. *Martial Arts of the Orient*. London: The Hamlyn Publishing Group Limited, 1975.

Yamaguchi, Norimi Gosei. *The Fundamentals of Goju-Ryu Karate*. Los Angeles: Ohara Publications, 1972.

Yanagi, Soetsu. *The Unknown Craftsman, A Japanese Insight into Beauty*. Tokyo: Kodansha International, Ltd., 1966.

Yu-Lan, Fung. *A Short History of Chinese Philosophy*. New York: The Macmillan Company, 1948.

Ware, James R. (Translator). *The Sayings of Mencius*. New York: New American Library, 1960.

Wilson, William Scott (Translator). *Budoshoshinshu: The Warrior's Primer of Daidoji Yuzan*. Burbank: Ohara Publications, Incorporated, 1984.

_____. *Ideals of the Samurai, Writings of Japanese Warriors*. 1982.

Photographs

Osamu Ozawa, 1 - (Archives of Randall Hassell)

Okinawan Masters, 6 - (Archives of Jose M. Fraguas)

Chosin Chibana, 8 - (Archives of Jose M. Fraguas)

Masatoshi Nakayama, 13 - (Archives of Jose M. Fraguas)

Morio Higaonna, 19, 48, 58 - (Courtesy of Jose M. Fraguas)

Gichin Funakoshi, 21 - (Archives of Jose M. Fraguas)

JKA Group, Tokyo, Japan, 22 - (Archives of Jose M. Fraguas)

Tsuguo Sakumoto, 36 - (Courtesy of Jose M. Fraguas)

Toshiaki Maeda, 38 - (Courtesy of Jose M. Fraguas)

Masahiro Okada, 41, 51 - (Courtesy of Jose M. Fraguas)

Teruo Chinen, 44, 68, 76 - (Courtesy of Jose M. Fraguas)

Choju Hentona, 47, 70 - (Courtesy of Jose M. Fraguas)

M. Gustavson & Steven Casper, 53 -
(Courtesy of Markus Boesch)

Randall Hassell, 56, 112 - (Courtesy of Jose M. Fraguas)

Y. Konishi, 63, 75 - (Courtesy of Jose M. Fraguas)

Yashunari Ishimi, 72 - (Courtesy of Jose M. Fraguas)

James Yabe, 78, 81 - (Courtesy of Jose M. Fraguas)

Les Safar, 82, 84 - (Courtesy of Jose M. Fraguas)

Hiroshi Shirai, 86, 91 - (Courtesy of Don Warrener)

Takeshi Oishi, 89 - (Archives of Jose M. Fraguas)

Masatoshi Nakayama, 97, 100, 105, 108, 110 -
(Courtesy of Tom Openlander)